Secrets of the Gnomes

Secrets of the

Rien Poortvliet

Harry N. Abrams, Inc., Publishers
Ballantine Books
New York

Gnomes

With text by Wil Huygen

Library of Congress Cataloging in Publication Data

Huygen, Wil.
    Secrets of the gnomes.

    Translation of: De oproep der kabouters.
    Sequel to: Gnomes.
    Summary: An account of the life and work of gnomes,
based on first-hand observations by the author and artist, who,
themselves turned into gnomes, visited with gnomes in
Lapland and Siberia.
    [1. Fairies—Fiction. 2. Fantasy] I. Poortvliet,
Rien, ill. II. Title.
PT5881.18.U9O613   839.3′186407   82-3948
ISBN 0-8109-1614-2   AACR2
ISBN 0-345-30861-1 (pbk)

Originally published under the title *De Oproep der Kabouters*
© 1981 Rien Poortvliet/Unieboek BV—Van Holkema &
Warendorf, Bussum, Netherlands
English translation © 1982 Unieboek BV—Van Holkema &
Warendorf, Bussum, Netherlands

Hardcover published in 1982 by Harry N. Abrams,
Incorporated, New York
Trade paperback published in 1984 in the United States by
Ballantine Books, a division of Random House, Inc., New York,
and simultaneously in Canada by Random House of Canada
Limited, Toronto, Canada

Printed and bound in the United States of America

early five years had passed since we first ventured into the world of gnomes, although this time the journey was not of our own choosing but because of a summons from the gnomes themselves. It seems that when compiling *Gnomes*, our first book, we had been too superficial in our presentation of the facts, even though the gnomes themselves had kept an eye on the work and had even consented to its publication.

Anyway, they wanted to meet us far from home in order to observe and test us. Once again—the more we saw of them, the more we realized how advanced they are. They have their roots in an older and more perfect world than ours, and they listen to voices that we have neither heard nor shall ever hear. Their observation of nature goes discouragingly further than ours and they have retained a dimension that we cannot even begin to

fathom; all we can do is merely guess about the realm of old and secret fairy tales.

At first the gnomes attempted to enlighten us with their usual gentleness by lifting a corner of the veil that hides everything unknown to us. Then, however, the situation became more of a challenge and resulted in their requesting us to deliver an urgent message, which is relayed in this book.

On the advice of Mirko, our host in Lapland, who allowed us to see parts of the *Secret Book*, we have illustrated everything precisely, although it was not always possible to make the invisible visible with pen or brush. We hope to have bridged the gap in the knowledge of gnomes—a presumption that we trust they will smilingly take for what it is worth.

THE JOURNEY TO LAPLAND

On the nineteenth of December of the Year of Our Lord 19—, we found tickets for a train journey to Kemijärvi in our mailbox, with stops at Bentheim, Bremen, Odense, Copenhagen, Stockholm, Haparanda, and Rovaniemi. In minute copperplate letters on snowy-white birch bark were the words:

Come, we have serious matters to discuss!

It could only be a message from the gnomes, and we could not ignore it. We were embarrassed to admit that we didn't know exactly where Kemijärvi was, but we soon found that it is in Finland near the Arctic Circle. The tickets were made out for the North-West Express leaving Utrecht on 20 December at 8:44 P.M. Lapland in winter? The thought was unsettling. What should we expect from the gnomes? We were none the wiser after a brief visit to the nearest gnome family in Soestduinen, Holland, who smiled amiably and nodded knowingly but gave nothing away.

On the evening of December 20 the North-West Express rumbled into the station at Utrecht on its way from Hoek of Holland to Sweden, and two minutes later we

were heading into the winter night for a two-day journey. We had drawing and writing materials as well as our
warmest clothing with us, but we wondered whether
they would be of any use at the Arctic Circle. In our ignorance we even imagined we could buy anything extra we
needed there! How different it turned out to be.

Nocturnal Holland slid past us. We stared with
heavy hearts as we left behind the snowy fields and
woods of our beloved Veluwe in our safe homeland.
After Bentheim we silently climbed into our bunks. Only
after the ferry-crossing to Korsør in Denmark did it begin
to get light outside and at 9:09 A.M. we entered the misty
city of Copenhagen. We had ten minutes to catch the
connection; soon afterward the train crossed to Hal-

singborg, Sweden. The weather was slightly better as we traveled the whole day through southern Sweden, the country over which Niels Holgersson had flown on the white goose Maarten—a thought that was unexpectedly comforting. We reached Stockholm at 5:44 P.M. Here we had to occupy ourselves until 9:10, when the night train to Haparanda departed. We had a bite to eat, and wandered around the town, visiting the town hall, the markets, and the Church of Saint Clara.

Traveling all night along the coast of the Baltic Sea, which is frozen for six months of the year, we noticed that the daylight hours were clearly shortening; only once did we see moose. We realized that there would be no more than three hours of daylight in Kemijärvi be-

cause of its proximity to the North Pole. We arrived at Haparanda at 5:40 the next afternoon. The train to Tornio took us from Sweden into Finland, where we then caught the train that would finally get us to Kemijärvi at 7:27. We passed tundras and went through vast forests of Christmas trees shrouded in darkness.

In our compartment, we stared listlessly out at the deep snow. The moon broke through from time to time and once in a while we saw a house or a cluster of buildings in a snowy field hedged by interlaced branches. There were a few passengers, and they were either reading or sleeping. In a corner sat a Lapp woman in colorful dress, holding on her knee a little girl who was drawing figures on the window with her index finger.

After leaving Haparanda the wind had increased to a storm. Somewhere between Rovaniemi and Kemijärvi the train came to a jolting, screeching halt and we were given to understand that an overhead wire had fallen. Although the repair team was on its way, passengers could expect a couple of hours of delay. It was almost half past seven. Fortunately, we still had some rolls left. It was bitterly cold outside—the wind howled and the windows were misted over.

After some time the conductor, a small wizened chap with a wrinkled, yellowish face and jet-black hair, came into our compartment. Earlier we had noticed him deliberately taking stock of us. His dark, slanting eyes somehow reflected the boundlessness of this land. He motioned us into the corridor outside the compartment where no one could hear us.

"Excuse me, gentlemen," he said in broken English. "I am a Lapp. I have traveled the world, but I have retained the ability to pick up messages from afar, like most of my people. I know who you are. You were to receive instructions upon arrival in Kemijärvi to walk back along the railroad track to a small church and wait there. Now that we are delayed anyway, you might just as well get out and walk up to the church from here. If you stay between the rails the snow will be less of a hindrance. I shall help you out of the train without being seen."

So that was the plan we were to follow! It helped to relieve our uneasiness about the immediate future. In the dark, we followed him to the front of the train where he helped us with our luggage. We thanked him, allowed our tips to be returned to us, and started off into the darkness. The safe, cosy, well-lit train got smaller and smaller behind us. There we were in the midst of gigantic rustling forests, stepping over the sleepers of the railway line in northern Finland, making for an unknown point, and not having any idea of what we were doing there!

Shortly afterward we saw the train with the repair-men approaching, and as we preferred not to be seen, we hid behind some bushes in the deep snow. They passed us by and thus unobserved we resumed our journey. A few miles farther we could see a small church some way from the track. We trudged toward it. Everything was peaceful. It was beastly cold, but the storm had died down as quickly as it had come up. The snow was at least three feet deep. The starry sky stretched above us and there was an ominous silence.

We waited ten minutes but nothing happened. Were we too early? After waiting another quarter of an hour we walked around the church and vicarage. There were no lights in the back or the front. A feeling of panic began to take hold of us. What had we let ourselves in for? Was this some sinister joke taken seriously by two gullible fools?

Then, suddenly, in spite of the darkness, we caught sight of an old gray-bearded Lapp, standing stock-still next to a road sign. With his thumb he was pointing over his shoulder toward the forest. At last, here were fresh instructions! New courage seemed to course through our veins and we strode past him in the direction he had indicated.

Our search was brief, however, for between the trees, at the edge of the forest, was a sleigh drawn by two reindeer. We were mystified: there was no driver! Once more we passed into the secret world of the gnomes. The reindeer snorted and pawed with their broad hooves. We got in and, snuggling under a voluminous sheepskin, sped off.

We traveled for hours. The cold did not worry us and the reindeer were indefatigable in spite of the deep snow. It was dark but because of the stars and snow everything was vaguely visible. One moment we were speeding through low birch and spruce woods, then gliding over tundralike plains with withered willows, dwarf birches, and brambles. We crossed many frozen rivers. The reindeer seemed to be following a definite course and never hesitated, although we saw nothing to mark the way. Only once did they let the sleigh come to a standstill; they stood motionless with their noses to the wind. The following moment they turned in unison sharp left and were off at a gallop, only to bear gently right in a mile-wide swoop and return to their original course. A little farther on we saw the reason for this: a fat troll was lumbering over the plain. As we passed him at a safe distance, he stood still and followed our progress. The reindeer continued to gallop for a few minutes and then fell back into a trot. We got an awful shock when an enormous branch, heavily laden with snow, came down just behind us with an earsplitting crash.

Reindeer have broad hooves that enable them to walk on snow and marshy ground. Their name comes from the old Norwegian hreindýri, and the Latin name is Rangifer tarandus. They are to be found in the whole tundra- and northern-forest zones of Europe, Asia, and North America, as well as in Spitsbergen (north of Norway), Greenland, and Nova-Zembla (Russia). In North America they are called caribou and are more heavily built. Males and females carry big, irregularly branched antlers that are shed in January, after which new ones grow. They reach almost seven feet in length and almost five feet in height. Color: brown in summer, grayish white in winter. They are excellent swimmers and tireless trotters whose hooves click when

they are on the move. The sleigh has to be some way from the animal because their droppings fall far behind them when in full gallop. They live in a wild or in a domesticated state. During the rutting season in September and October the old solitary bulls surround themselves with females. Twenty-eight to thirty-four weeks later a calf is born and becomes fully grown in a year. Reindeer are day creatures that feed on reindeer moss, grass, herbs, buds, and bark. Domesticated reindeer (especially in Siberia and Lapland) always live outdoors in herds; they are left to themselves and are followed by man when their great "trek" begins. Their greatest enemy is the wolf. In the Arctic, reindeer are of supreme importance to man. In their wild state they are mainly used for meat, and when tamed they supply many of man's basic needs: food—meat and milk (22% fat, 11% albumen, 3.5% sugar); clothing—hides, wool, needles (bone), and thread. They can be used for pulling, carrying, or riding. Below −40° F. it would be deadly for a man to breathe through his mouth—even then air exhaled through the nostrils will freeze on his upper lip. But reindeer can keep trotting for hours at a temperature of −65° F. As draft animals they are prone to whims, but a wise driver can handle them easily. He uses a long pole as a driving unit with which he only has to touch the reindeer lightly to keep them moving.

Suddenly we heard a faint sound as if a single note were being blown on a horn. The nearer we got, the louder it became. We came to a small clearing in the spruce and birch wood, where the reindeer stopped and stared to the right toward the sound. Our hearts leapt. After all the tedium, worry, and uncertainty of the journey, there was an old and trusted sight: a gnome standing on a tree trunk. He was blowing an immensely long horn, but when he saw us he stopped and walked toward the sleigh. Climbing onto it he said, "Good evening. Welcome! I was just blowing the Midwintertune,* as today is Sunturn. I am Mirko, and for the time being I will be your host. Marvelous that you came so quickly. Please get out."

In no time at all, he had unharnessed the reindeer. It was astonishing to see him untie the frozen leather straps so deftly with his tiny hands. He did not want us to help him and when we were about to take our suitcases out he said with a wink, "Leave them there. We have no thieves here."

Mirko had given the reindeer some yellow biscuits that they crunched crisply before calmly walking off and disappearing among the trees. We glanced at each other. The moment had arrived when we would be told why the gnomes wanted us, we thought. Did they want to honor us or punish us? We managed to say nothing in spite of our curiosity and followed Mirko to a small hut under the trees. It turned out to be a sauna. A glowing stove stood in the corner. "This is a deserted sauna," Mirko said, "that once belonged to forest workers. I fixed it up a bit. You must be tired. Go in it for an hour and rest. After that you must sleep." As we undressed he

* The purpose of the Midwintertune in the twelve nights around Christmas is to keep bad spirits at bay as well as the Wolf Riders of the Wild Hunt.

doused the hot stones on the stove with water at an enormous rate. Thick steam resulted and the heat rose alarmingly. We stretched out on the wooden benches and allowed him to splash us now and then with cold water and to beat us with birch twigs. He didn't seem to mind the heat at all. The speed and vigor with which it all happened is only to be found among gnomes. After an hour he said, "Now outside into the snow! Roll around and around, but not for too long since you aren't used to it."

We did it and somehow managed to come out alive. It felt fantastic. When we returned indoors the weariness in our limbs had disappeared. Instead we felt a heavy languor. Mirko had let most of the heat out of the hut. Two steaming plates with wooden spoons were waiting on one of the wooden benches. "Mushrooms in reindeer cream," our host said. "Enjoy your meal and then try to sleep."

He vanished through a vertical split between the boards above the skirting. We emptied the plates. We had never tasted anything like it. Everything that light, air, sun, moon, and earth could produce seemed to be in it. Then we stretched out on the benches and fell into a deep slumber.

When we woke up it was either still dark or dark again. The shadowy beamed ceiling of the cabin was miles above us and the bench seemed to be an immense wooden plain. We heard a voice: "My apologies. I should have warned you, but I found it more amusing like this. You must understand that it was necessary. Besides, it is an honor accorded to very few humans: Jules Verne for example, Hans Christian Andersen, and of course the Grimm Brothers."

We sat up and gazed into the half-serious, half-laughing eyes of Mirko. He stood behind us on the bench and all of a sudden we realized that we were as small as he was! After the initial shock, we burst out laughing. We had pointed green caps on, green smocks and trousers, and we wore felt boots. Not only were we as small as a gnome, but we had their proportions, complete with tummy, heavy torso, and big head, and *we could see in the dark just as if it were light, not to mention the fact that we smelled every detail around us as if everything had a strong aroma.*

"This is the guest attire," Mirko said. "You will feel perfectly comfortable in it." He showed us a gilt-edged, leatherbound book that he had been hiding behind his back plus our drawing and writing things, all of which were reduced in size. "Jot down everything that happens to you from now on into this," he said simply, handing us the book, which had a little golden lock. Inside we found blank sheets in loose quires.

The hut creaked as outside the wind howled through the trees. The storm had returned in full force.

From now on we will occasionally interrupt our travelogue with details of the customs, household objects, machines, and other secrets we came across in gnomeland.

NEW YEAR AT THE ARCTIC CIRCLE

"Follow me," Mirko said amiably, as he sprang off the bench. We hesitated a moment because of the enormous height, but once we dared to jump we landed lightly and painlessly. The split through which Mirko had vanished a few hours ago had appeared no bigger than a rat hole, but now we could walk through it standing upright. Beyond it was a dark passage. "This connects my house with the sauna cabin," Mirko said, taking a lantern from the wall and deftly lighting the candle with a tinder. "It is 330 feet long; we'll be there in no time. We could have gone above ground but without cross-country skis we couldn't go far in this fresh snow, and I've left them at home. Anyway, in this storm there is the danger of falling branches."

Because of the reduced gravity, we found moving just as easy as we had found jumping. Not only absolutely but also relatively we were lighter: our body content had diminished three times, our body surface twice.

Finally we were led through a door jammed between two tree roots and into another passage. We could hear from the sound of the raging storm that the passage to the right ended in the open air. Mirko opened the doors

of wall cupboards that contained all kinds of skis. "If we go out, choose a pair. They are indispensable in fresh snow. I made them all myself."

We took a passage to the left. There was no polecat trap, as we expected. A little farther on we came across a revolving door trimmed with most peculiar brushes. "Hair of the woolly rhinoceros," Mirko muttered as he turned it. "They have been extinct for the last ten thousand years. Nothing that creeps or has four legs can get through here. My house is built under a cluster of rocks because the woolly rhinos and mammoths used to destroy an awful lot. This house is thirty thousand years old. I shall let you see a map that shows the movement of the animals as far as England."

We asked him how he got hold of the hair if the animals died out so long ago.

"Wait, wait. That will soon be clear," said our host.

Finally the passage ended with a few stairs at a copper door that led into a boot room. Inside was a rather crudely painted hope chest and another door.

Mirko knocked on it significantly. "Just you wait," he said.

A   snowplow
B   earmuffs
C   skis
D   boot room
E   hope chest
F   tube cakes
G   bathroom
H   pump
I   drainage pipe
J   hearth
K   air duct

L   hand-held cleaver
M   sauna
N   sleeping alcoves
O   firewood
P   attic
Q   rocking-chair cradle
R   lemmings
S   carved wooden "cock's tail"

Snowplow made to resemble the snow flea (<u>Entomobia nivalis</u>), an ancient insect one and a half millimeters long, that drills its way through snow in a similar fashion.

In weather below -4° F, gnomes wear earmuffs knitted from the hair of the woolly rhinoceros or the reindeer.

Their extremely keen sense of hearing is hampered by the earmuffs, and consequently they don't go as far away on their winter trips. In still colder regions, such as Siberia, they wear arctic caps made out of mammoth hair and with these the gnomes can face temperatures as low as -70° F. Their appearance is made very grim by these caps, and this is also an advantage.

Tube cakes (one half whole wheat and one half white flour) are made by pressing a hole into the dough with a mold.

The center part is used as a bun.

Gnome women have historically been better at this job than the men.

The hand-held wood cleaver nailed to the wall; the knife is so sharp that it slices through wood like butter.

The rocking-chair cradle is made exclusively for twins. One problem is getting up unnoticed once the babies have been rocked to sleep.

Without having to fuss with paper or kindling, gnomes can make a dependable little fire within two minutes by means of "rooster-cuts" in the wood. Larch wood produces the most beautiful curls. Christmas ornaments are made according to the same principle.

For a pet the gnomes keep the lemming, or reindeer mouse, an arctic rodent of the family of the field voles (Cricetidae).

When overpopulation occurs (every 8-10 years), these animals go on mass migrations, always from high to low-lying terrain, during which great numbers die as victims of predators and drowning. They do not hibernate.

We were puzzled but thought it better left as it was.

"Another guest was to have come this evening," resumed Mirko. "But I think this storm is too much for even him."

We went to the table. Everything happened here with a timeless rhythm, it seemed, and the fare set before us was a dream. We held hands.* There were parasol mushrooms, chanterelles, spice cakes, mountain raspberries, bilberries, red whortleberries, sour cream and hazelnuts, and yellow Chinese tea.

"How can you get hold of all this in the winter?" we asked.

"That is what our cooling space is for," said Mirko.

Elsa scolded a lemming that was gnawing on a Christmas decoration. "The Lapps call lemmings reindeer mice," laughed Mirko. "Lemmings are all nibblers."

Every now and then the house trembled. "There is a tearing snowstorm," said Mirko, pointing upward. "If you were to go out now, you would risk being found hundreds of yards from here after the storm. Our visitor will have to seek shelter whether he wants to or not." Having said this, our host became absorbed in thought.

(travelogue continued)

Mirko slipped past us through the second door into the living room, and we followed. An ancient smell of resin filled the room, and candles flickered. Two lemmings were playing on the floor and we saw a cleverly designed rocking-chair cradle. Mirko took a pretty female gnome by the hand and said, "May I introduce Elsa?"

She could not have been more than 110 years old, as was Mirko. "How nice to see you in person!" she said.

There was a festive atmosphere, rather like home when visitors are expected for the holidays. Two adorable babies lay in the cradle, and they laughed when we tickled them. "Pretty children," we said.

"They are Milo and Annie," Elsa said tenderly. "We'll soon go to the table. Just sit quietly for a while, then we'll have tea."

As he filled his pipe Mirko remarked, "It is almost Christmas for you people. Yesterday was Sunturn, the lowest rise of the sun, thus the shortest day, although that is actually on the twenty-first of December." He regarded us mysteriously as he said, "We still have four days left!"

* Before every meal, the gnomes hold each other's hands and silently wish each other a successful meal.

The cuckoo clock struck 11:00 A.M., but time here did not seem to exist. We still sat cosily smoking at the table.

"One game and then to bed," said Mirko. He rose and turned back the carpet. A huge gooseboard* was drawn on the floor, but instead of geese there were dinosaurs; instead of a prison was a troll's den; instead of a well was a floating iceberg. The pawns used in the game were bronze figures of prehistoric animals and the ivory dice were from mammoth tusks. Everything was decorated with secret markings, scrolls, and flowers. The

* A gooseboard is used in a dice game for children in Holland.

chips were lumps of gold. We had played two games when Mirko announced: "And now to bed! Slitzweitz."

We were surprised to see a well-known portrait when he opened the doors of the sleeping alcove. Mirko must have found a postage stamp in one of our pockets and hung it up out of kindness.

Then the moment came to go to the bathroom. Inside, a music box played a lively trepak, a cossack dance in 2/4 time that was very amusing. The seat was beautifully painted and quite comfortable.

Elsa breast-fed her babies while we undressed, as if this was the most natural thing in the world, which of course it is.

Playing games is one way
the gnomes keep fit:
tilt at the ring
is not as easy
as it looks,
and teaches
a gnome
dexterity
in dense
undergrowth;

sack-racing
is a favorite
(and useful);

races for the advanced
are held in high grass
to make it more
difficult.

Leapfrog cannot be played
sideways because of the
pointed caps, and
the ♀ have to take
their skirts off.

Walking on stilts greatly improves the sense of balance

(the stilts measuring up to three feet).

Ice quoits keeps the sense of spacial judgment on the mark.

Through all of this, the gnome has preserved his childlike quality (which also serves to fool trolls).

Making shadows on the wall adds excitement to fairy tales for the children.

to see which end turns upward. In that side a hole is bored that holds the wick. Finally the chestnut is placed in a bowl of water and the wick is lit. It can burn for twelve hours.)

We called "Slitzweitz" again and closed the alcove doors behind us. The air was quite fresh for being so deep in the rocks. The house still shook in the storm but here below it was warm and safe. We discussed what had happened to us and guessed how long it would be before we knew what the gnomes wanted next. On one hand it seemed as though we had lived here for years, but on the other we had a growing sense of alarm as to how we would ever regain our normal size. As it was, we just had to have faith in the gnomes. It was as it was, and we were being shown things of which no other living soul would dream. For the time being we began drawing some of our experiences to this point, and that filled up the first thirty pages in the book that Mirko gave us.

In front of the alcove was a basket of birch twigs, which turned out to be disposable toothbrushes. A sharpened point on one end of the birch twig serves as a toothpick; the other end when chewed can be used as a toothbrush. A wick in a chestnut lit up the alcove. (With a thick needle a number of holes are made in a chestnut, which is then left in oil for a day. Later it is put into water

The blue print is made with indigo-drenched linen on which figures have first been drawn in wax or loam. The dye is absorbed by the linen fibers except where they are covered with wax or loam. Here they remain uncolored.

This is called negative blue print (white on blue), which is more beautiful than vice versa.

In Europe, indigo was made from the woad plant (Isatis tinctoria). The powder starts off red and becomes blue when exposed to the air, through oxidation.

Finnish gnome costumes for everyday wear and for Sundays.

Elimäki

Koillismaa

Sakkola Rautu

Kuorebesi

Kirkkonummi

Parikkala

Pukkila

Tuuteri

The scarf is also festive.

Muff and shawl come out of the closet when the weather calls for them.

During extreme cold spells
a cape is worn.
↙

Nor can the male
gnome go without
earmuffs. ↗

In the winter,
long underwear is essential.
↙
↘

For the female
less clothing
is necessary
in the
summer.
←

Simple but decorative,
printed night things are
the usual sleeping attire.

nightgown   nightshirt
↓   ↓

(notice the
mustache holder) ↗

The gnomes construct their water-supply installations in rocky terrain by means of huge drill units (discussed later). They choose two lakes on slightly different levels. When the house has been drilled out they make a vertical passage below it.

Before digging the horizontal passage that is to join the two lakes at a great depth, they sink a tarpaulin in both lakes where the rock drill will strike the lake bed.

The drill bores a passage, first to the lower lake and then to the upper one. As soon as it breaks through the floor of the lake, the tarpaulins are pressed against the floor by suction so that only a small amount of water seeps into the bore holes. The drill is then removed and a pump is placed at the top of the house. At this stage the tarpaulins are removed and the water streams by from high to low. A fine meshed hive is placed over the hole in the upper lake to prevent blockage by mud or sludge. Usually the lakes are clean enough to be used for drinking water. If this is not the case, nitrogen cylinders that extract the dirt and bacteria are installed in the upper passage. These cylinders can be changed by means of an ordinary diving bell that the gnomes use for their other lake bed investigations. The constant stream ensures fresh water.

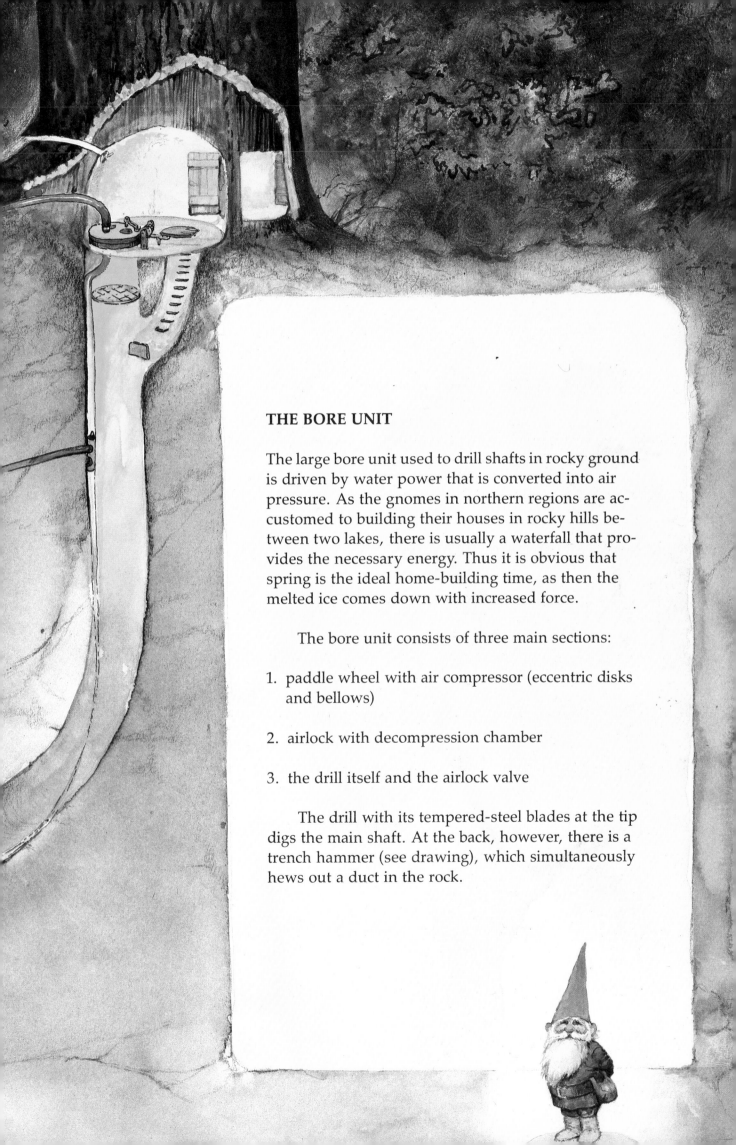

THE BORE UNIT

The large bore unit used to drill shafts in rocky ground is driven by water power that is converted into air pressure. As the gnomes in northern regions are accustomed to building their houses in rocky hills between two lakes, there is usually a waterfall that provides the necessary energy. Thus it is obvious that spring is the ideal home-building time, as then the melted ice comes down with increased force.

The bore unit consists of three main sections:

1. paddle wheel with air compressor (eccentric disks and bellows)

2. airlock with decompression chamber

3. the drill itself and the airlock valve

The drill with its tempered-steel blades at the tip digs the main shaft. At the back, however, there is a trench hammer (see drawing), which simultaneously hews out a duct in the rock.

AIR COMPRESSOR

By means of a paddle wheel at the foot of a waterfall, the water energy is transferred to the camshaft with eccentric disks (A), and thence by way of the propelling rods (B), onto the yokes (C), which are connected to each other by a common shaft (D). The yokes move the membranes of the bellows (E) up and down, thus producing air pressure without any pollution. This can only be achieved by using the one-way air passage suction valve holes. (The development of this mechanism probably led to the creation of the *Rommelpot*, an old, western European musical instrument made of a jug and a pig's bladder.)

The air compressed in the bellows goes via the air pipe (G) and the second hole (N2) of the wooden distributor (see Airlock) to the large bore shaft, resulting in high atmospheric pressure while work is in progress.

AIRLOCK WITH DECOMPRESSION CHAMBER

In the airlock there is a wooden distributor (H) with holes N1 and N2, which can be maneuvered by means of the cogged bar (M). When at rest the air goes through opening N1, when in operation through opening N2. The illustration shows it at rest. To keep the pressure in the lock constant, a regulating valve (K) has been introduced. Next to the lock chamber is a decompression chamber (L) by which the gnomes enter and leave. The adjustable sliding scuttle (J) is situated in the channel or duct, and this enables the grit to be removed to the outside under the waterfall.

In the duct next to the main shaft is a rope (green) connected to a bell in the lock chamber that allows the gnomes to sound an alarm or simply signal a request to be pulled up for food or to sign off for the day.

The contraption on the parachute lift serves to stop the lift at any desired point in the shaft.

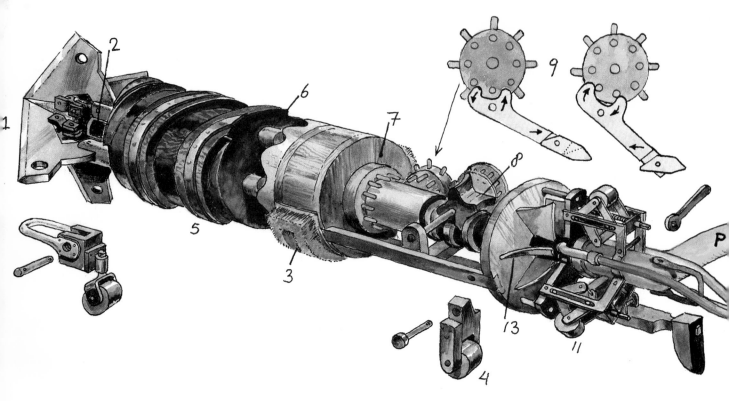

DRILLING MACHINE

The tempered-steel blades (1) do the actual digging and hewing. The effective cooling of the waste compressed air prevents their becoming overheated. The grit loosened by the blades is removed via the upper suction channel (2) and the lower, brush-lined suction channel (3) to the pipe (P) and then via the duct to the scuttle (J) outside. When not in use, the drill can be moved on the coasters (4). After the preliminary work of the tempered-steel blades, the walls of the main shaft are smoothed by walnut rollers with steel grinding strips (5).

The hammer cogs (6) get the power from the cam unit (7). The shape of the cam unit causes a revolving hammer motion to the hammer cogs, turning the entire foremost part of the drill and resulting in the notching stroke of the blades. In order to reduce the revolutions, thus increasing the power of the blades, cog-wheel-reduction is applied (8). The drill is pushed slowly forward during drilling with the help of the creeping cog (9).

Naturally the energy for all this is obtained from the compressed air, which is conveyed through the red jet tubing previously mentioned (10) or (O) to make the propeller (13) rotate, which in turn passes the revolving motion forward by means of a corkscrew shaft. The insertion wheel (11) is added to make underground bends negotiable.

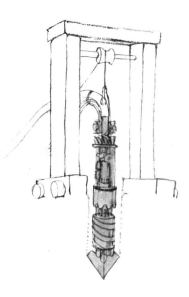

LOCK DOOR

The round, barrel-shaped lock door is situated under the main shaft. A normal rectangular door is built into it. The high pressure in the main shaft passes through the lock by means of the three red jet tubes of the compressed air supply (O), which is then conducted to the actual bore units. The turnvalve (Q) serves to shut off the shaft or duct.

While the rectangular door in the round lock door remains closed, the compressed air is forced to find its way through the red tubes (O). If the door is opened the pressure in the tubes disappears and the machine stops. Back through the lock door goes the tube for grit removal

(P), which connects by means of a bayonet mount (R) with the side duct. This duct is covered over with duct-covering planks (S). The grit is removed by the spent pressure in reverse from the machine and is conducted back via the channel (P).

To prevent the lock door from slipping off into the depths during vertical drilling, the expansion bar contraption (T) has been invented, by means of which the whole lock door can be jammed in the curve of the shaft wall.

This is how the situation can be at any given moment: the parachute lift is at the bottom of the shaft just behind the round lock door. The drill is working at full capacity.

The grit is being removed via the duct and the scuttle and is taken outside.

The midnight break arrives, and the gnomes down below want to come up. They open the rectangular door that cuts off the air pressure from the machine, causing it to stop. Then they lift up a duct plank and pull on the rope that jingles the bell up above. The plank is then replaced.

The gnome engineer above turns the distributor with the cog bar so that the compressed air no longer gets into the main shaft but goes via the hole N1 into the duct. At the same time he lowers the scuttle so that the compressed air does not escape through the gravel-removal tube, but goes straight down and blows the whole duct clean. This air reverses at the bottom of the shaft and comes up via the main shaft, blowing the parachute lift up in front of it. Alas, this is not done without creating a cloud of dust that fortunately does not last long. The gnomes get out, climb the ladder to the air lock, and leave their work site via the decompression chamber.

A

D

C

B

E

G

HAND DRILL FOR SMALLER JOBS

The up-and-down lever motion of two gnomes is converted by the pawls into a one-way rotation. The grit that has been loosened deep down is blown by the compressed air inlet (A) to the drill-grit waste pipe (B) and removed. The lid (C), drawn above for clarity, is supposed to rest on the drill hole. The drill can reach any desired depth by means of additional extension pieces (E) and the air-supply hole (G).

CAVE ENLARGER

The cave enlarger is an axle to which chains with iron
balls are attached; a rotating motion causes a
formidable bombardment of the rock face.
The gnomes make little of the seeming
labor hazards of this machine.

The construction of the interior
of the rocky hollow begins after all
the drilling has been done and the
unit has been collected above ground by the contractor.
The wood for the house is loosely positioned
<u>outside</u> so that it can be permanently assembled
within.

First, however, the tarpaulins
are withdrawn from the drill
holes and pulled up so that the water can
flow freely between the lakes

Gnomes know exactly where Mother Nature can spare a tree...

and how to hew it.

fall wedge

first wedge

For an ax to be wieldable it should reach from the ground to the navel (this does not apply to humans).

To obtain a straight surface on the trunk, a chalked string is pulled taut lengthwise. By pulling up the string and letting it snap back, a neat chalk line is made that indicates where the gnome must cut. →

He uses an ordinary ax for the rough profile.

As side straighteners, adz and

drawknife are used.

Father and son help each other saw the trunk to size.

From time to time the teeth have to be pushed outward with a saw set.

For the so-called semicircular joint, the trunk is sawed to different depths and the curve is chiseled out.

Pulleys are favored
for transporting
wood.

The ornamental rods
are turned by means
of a swaying Larix branch.

He does the sawing and notching to size of the biggest logs where the trees are felled (usually near his parents' house).

Then he transports them,
gliding →
← pulling
or
floating.
↓

The smaller wood is transported overland, using every path and animal track the gnome comes across.

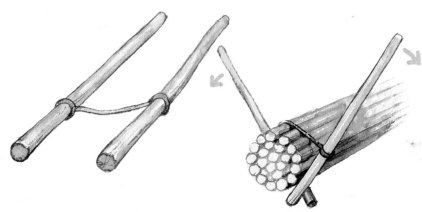

Fine poles are tied in a bundle, the so-called marling hitch.

When the building material arrives at the site of the house-to-be, the gnome pulls it in immediately so he can insert a revolving door (edged with brushes of the woolly rhinoceros)

in order to keep out undesirables (like vipers)

To begin with, he puts out a couple of squatters.

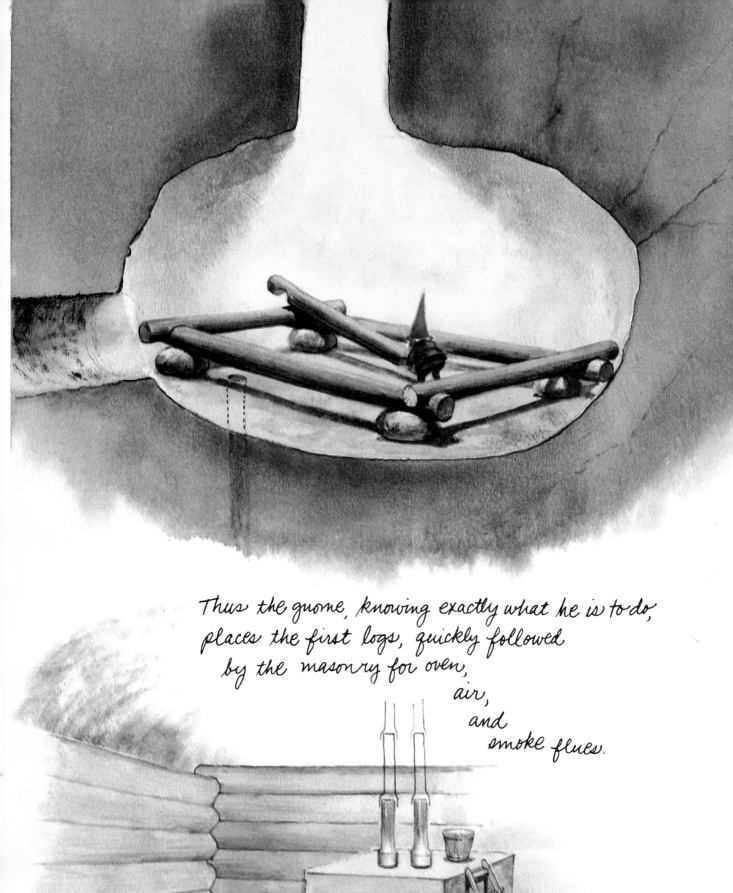

Thus the gnome, knowing exactly what he is to do,
places the first logs, quickly followed
by the masonry for oven,
air,
and
smoke flues.

beer offered
to the →
house
builders

The Housewarming Party

A bride is not allowed to see the new house before her marriage.
The parents of the bride and groom inspect the house when it is
ready. The bride's father brings a wine-colored chest under his
arm that he does not hand over until he has conducted a
thorough inspection of the locks, masonry, carpentry products,
the quality of the furnishings, etc,
and has found them to his liking.
The chest contains earth from the
immediate surroundings of the
bride's home. If the father of the
bride is satisfied with everything,
the chest is cemented into one of
the walls and the deal is clinched.

THE EMOTIONAL LIFE OF THE GNOME

A gnome is so close to nature that he is always making friends and acquaintances, which must be very pleasant. He likes everything and everybody. He is used to giving. He doesn't ask for what he gets as a matter of course, such as love, affection, or material things. A gnome knows no fear, but is precautious and knows when to get out of the way. He has an inborn feeling of security. This is hereditary, but is, to no mean degree, strengthened by the way his mother enfolds him from the time of his birth, namely by the completely natural use of cuddle circles.

Here are some examples of cuddle circles that exert a positive influence throughout the entire life of a gnome.

It is by no means limited to only mother-child relationships; father-child or other combinations are just as good!

It's easy to sum up: just as much love and tenderness as is poured into a child is returned to others throughout his life. A feeling of security and of being one with earth and cosmos results in the so-called cosmic-telluric attachment, which is seldom found in humans. It has nothing to do with being brave or not brave—quite the contrary: because gnomes operate from a safe basis, their physical and mental capacity is at a maximum. They never panic. Just as other beings, the gnome must have developed his emotions via his sense of touch.

TOUCH
From birth the sense of touch is responsible for the first observations, awareness, and knowledge. All other senses have evolved

from this one. It is very stupid to answer a child's enquiry "What is that?" with "That is for leaving alone." A child has to have an object in his hands to know for the rest of his life what the object really represents.

Touch is thus the organ of knowledge. Touch lies in the wrapping of the body—the skin. The mouth is extremely important to children for touching and discovering purposes. In the beginning touch transmits messages that are registered and catalogued within. As feelings and emotions are built up over the years, touch no longer only receives but also gives out sympathy, comfort, tenderness, and love.

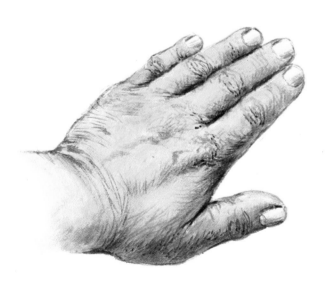

THE HAND
To beings blessed with reason, the hand is the ideal instrument with which to feel. A maximum of touch qualities and expressive possibilities are centered in the hands, and it is a part of the body with inconceivable versatility. Moreover, gesticulations and the offering and shaking of a hand nearly always have an emotional meaning.

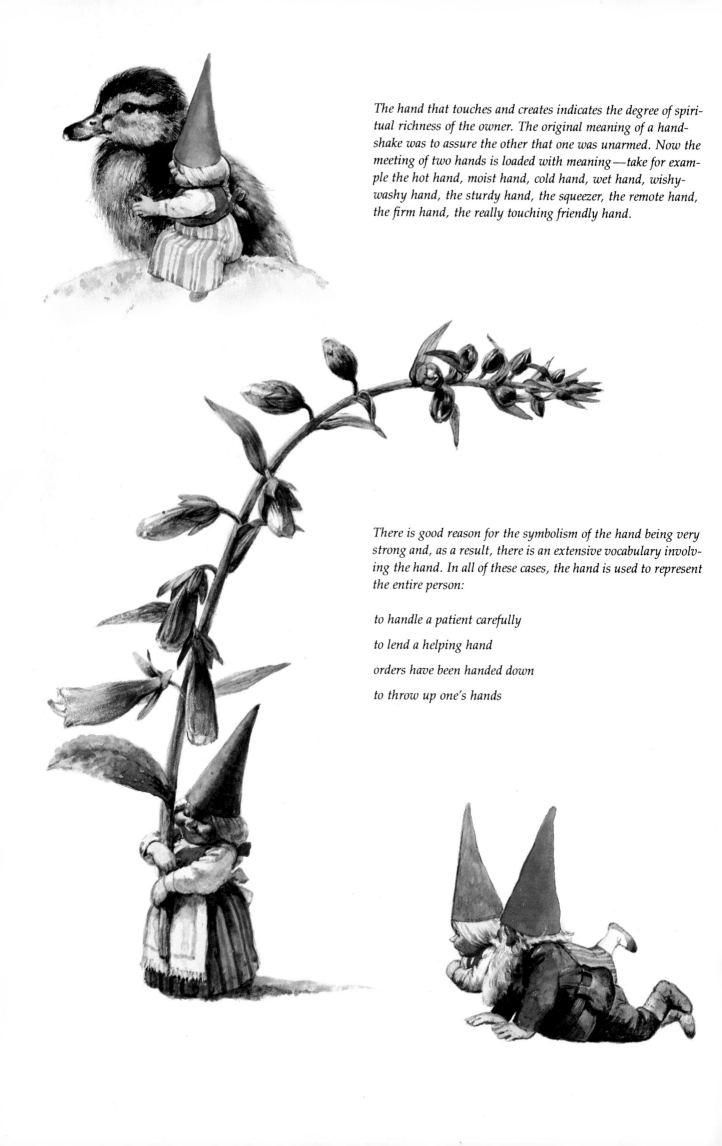

The hand that touches and creates indicates the degree of spiritual richness of the owner. The original meaning of a handshake was to assure the other that one was unarmed. Now the meeting of two hands is loaded with meaning—take for example the hot hand, moist hand, cold hand, wet hand, wishy-washy hand, the sturdy hand, the squeezer, the remote hand, the firm hand, the really touching friendly hand.

There is good reason for the symbolism of the hand being very strong and, as a result, there is an extensive vocabulary involving the hand. In all of these cases, the hand is used to represent the entire person:

to handle a patient carefully

to lend a helping hand

orders have been handed down

to throw up one's hands

The hand can also be strongly symbolic on its own:

an imploring hand

a blessing hand

a conjuring hand

the laying on of a healing hand

the handshake to seal the contract

a greeting hand

the extended hand

the protecting hand

with a rough hand

with a gentle hand

a searching or probing hand

with folded hands

the life-giving hand

Gnomes pat the trunks of trees and say "Hello brother tree," just as we pat a dog or the nose of a horse. (He does that too to any old animal.) From tenderness, love comes naturally. This applies to everything.*

* *Refer to I. Corinthians 13:4–7.*

TENDERNESS

Tenderness means—and imparts—warmth and respect. The whole hand expresses the quality of the meeting, not just the fingers, which express feeling without depth. Only the whole hand can encircle something tenderly. A small child (one who is frightened, for example) must be lifted by the encircling hands of someone squatting. This conveys a feeling of warmth and safety to the child. WRONG is: lifting while standing upright and leaning stiffly forward. Here the hand circumvention is missing and the high/low feeling is increased instead of reduced. A tender hand always gives, never takes. A caressing hand entices and takes. It has only sexual significance.

The harmony of nature has become so much a part of the gnomes that they can't make head nor tail of human aggression and cruelty. The Iron Curtain means nothing, nor does war, fratricide, theft, envy, struggle for power, or any other human misery. Should the backwash of human cruelty touch them directly, they simply step aside.

DISUNITY

Differences of opinion, irritation, and minor quarrels naturally do occur from time to time in gnome marriages. The usual solution is for the grieved party to sing the complaint in a self-made song, whereupon the guilty party usually starts laughing and acknowledges that he or she has been wrong.

If this fails, it becomes more serious. This method is then tried: for a solid fifteen minutes wife tells husband what she thinks of him. Husband may only answer the next day, when he will get equal time, and so forth. This usually solves everything.

Many a quarrel ends in a pleasant bath.

While the gnome boys are away from home copying the Secret Book, gnome girls are busy learning too. The girls learn how to handle all sorts of wounds and bone fractures in the veterinary hospital.

In the game reserves for threatened animal species nearly all the helpers are female gnomes. In the Bat Reserve near Ede, in Holland, for example, it is common knowledge that gnome women have been taken on as maternity and parasite specialists.

Patching the colors of damaged butterflies requires artistic craftsmanship.

Another life's work of female gnomes is the creation and up-keep of subterranean fishponds. These are huge grottoes containing lakes that are either natural or hewn into the rocks. Into the steep cliffsides around the lake, paths are chiseled out where lanterns and torches are hung. There are grottoes that narrow to small openings behind which new lakes can be found, even numbering as many as twelve, which is a fantastic sight in the flaring torchlight.

All fishes from prehistoric times up till today are preserved in these subterranean lakes. Some have phosphorescent bodies with all the colors of the rainbow; others have lighted fins and tails; still others have eyes like torches. All salt- and fresh-water fishes are represented, including deep sea fishes. Controlling the oxygen supply in seawater is quite a job.

If any species on earth is threatened with extinction it is extra specially cared for here.

The biggest and most complete fishponds are under the Ural Mountains· Huge underground waters also used for this purpose are under the Ardennes; in Norway; in the Balkans; and in the Rocky Mountains.

A sound in the living room awakened us and we opened the alcove doors. Elsa went by in her birthday suit on her way to the bathroom. Prudery does not exist among gnomes. Natural purity is the order of the day, just as it is with animals. The cuckoo clock struck six. When Elsa was finished we took turns in the bath, which was made all the cosier by the storm outside.

At breakfast Mirko said, "Our guest is not coming for the moment. He has sent a telepathic message." He continued thoughtfully: "The question is, what must I do now? He won't be here before the New Year."

What could the mysterious guest have to do with our visit to Lapland?

Mirko said with a laugh, "Don't think that you have come here for nothing. But I have agreed to wait for him before I . . . no, I'm not going to say it yet. First we must pay a visit to the woolly rhinos!"

Gnomes hurry only when necessary. Their patience is as boundless as that of animals. Hurrying through a meal is considered foolish and an insult to the hostess. Indeed, they live so long that there is plenty of time . . . and they live so long by taking plenty of time! Moreover, they savor every morsel with their extremely well-developed sense of smell and, consequently, of taste.

We began with soup that tasted like the smell of a sunny wild-strawberry-covered mountainside. Then Mirko said, "First, a tune!"

It is not unusual for gnomes to interrupt a meal for amusement. They believe that classical music has a character-forming influence on babies from birth. An ancient lullaby was sung that we later saw in original pointed-cap writing.

On returning to the breakfast table, we found we could eat relatively more than beforehand. As a result of our diminished size, our body surface was relatively bigger in contrast to content, and the rate of digestion increased.

Ancient Cradle Song of the Gnomes

Tuuti lasta, tuuti pientä,
tuuti lasta nukkumahan.
Laulan lasta nukkumahan
uuvutan unen rekehen;
käy unonen ottamahan,
kultaisehen korjahasi
hopiasehen rekehen!

Sleep little child, Sleep little one,
Sleep little child, fall asleep quickly.
I sing my little one to sleep
lull him to sleep in the sleigh of dreams;
come, sleep, hide him softly.
Son of sleep, come carry him away
secretly
in your golden cradle
in your silver sleigh!

At midnight, having spent more than four hours at the table, we left the house. Everything creaked in the wind and snowflakes tumbled in at the far end of the passage. We arrived in a long passage by way of the deserted, cold sauna.

"This passage was dug by the blind prehistoric mole,"* said Mirko. "He did not have a permanent home and was always digging around for females." Mirko increased his pace to a canter. After twenty minutes we paused to swallow a couple of caraway seeds.** New strength poured into our limbs and away we went.

After three quarters of an hour the passage sloped downward. It got colder. "Now we are in the permafrost," our host said, "the perpetually frozen earth. Watch now."

We stepped into an ice-cold, dimly lit space. Two enormous rust-colored hairy rhinos stood in front of us. A third lay in pieces on the ground. "They froze so instantaneously when they were overtaken by a snowstorm in the last ice age that the grass is still between their teeth," Mirko told us as we climbed onto their horns. "My father and grandfather hacked them free bit by bit. We use those pieces on the ground for fur and leather supply.

"The reason it is so light here is because of an ever-phosphorescent stone.*** In ancient times it was in a dragon's den in Norway. My grandfather built a couple in here."

*   *Talpa caeca borealis major*
**   *Fructus carum carvi*
*** *Lapis draconensis aureolucentis*

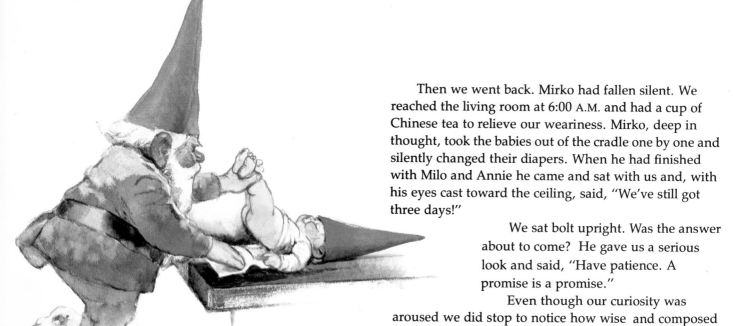

Then we went back. Mirko had fallen silent. We reached the living room at 6:00 A.M. and had a cup of Chinese tea to relieve our weariness. Mirko, deep in thought, took the babies out of the cradle one by one and silently changed their diapers. When he had finished with Milo and Annie he came and sat with us and, with his eyes cast toward the ceiling, said, "We've still got three days!"

We sat bolt upright. Was the answer about to come? He gave us a serious look and said, "Have patience. A promise is a promise."

Even though our curiosity was aroused we did stop to notice how wise and composed Mirko was, especially considering his youth.

We once again went to the table. Relaxed? Yes, that we had learned on our own, apart from the fact that we now had gnome attributes ourselves.

We then went to bed and slept from 10:00 A.M. till six that evening. The bitter Arctic wind shrieked over the plains and through the woods.

After breakfast we sat at the table for ages. It was Christmas Eve in the rest of the world. Somehow or other it was impossible to ask outright why we had been called from home in the middle of the winter. It was as if our tongues refused to do their duty. Perhaps it was because as gnomes we automatically knew what was expected of us.

When we left the table and were helping Elsa clear the dishes, Mirko stood gazing into the fire. We talked about the sea-bird disaster that had just occurred on the west coast of Sweden through the illegal spilling of oil, but Mirko's thoughts seemed to be elsewhere and he took no part in the conversation.

Suddenly he turned and strode to the boot room.

Through the half-open door we saw him open the lid of the hope chest and step inside. We were even more amazed when he began to go down and then totally disappeared.

Stairs squeaked and we could hear noises from below. Elsa too was excited and laughed shyly at us. Eventually we saw the point of our host's cap reappear above the hope chest. He had two books in his hand. One was enormous and the other was small. He stepped out of the chest, shut the lid with his elbow, and came back into the living room. There he laid the books on the table.

A green light glowed. Elsa began to blow all the candles out. When she was finished, the green radiance lay like a cloth over the table. The surrounding faces had a green glow. Mirko solemnly opened the largest book and said, "The time has come for you to peep into the Secret Book." He was silent for a moment, then went on: "These books contain everything the gnomes have recorded since the creation of the world—History, Rules of Living, Material Knowledge, etc. I wanted to wait until

our guest got here, as he has also something to say to you, but that cannot be for now. The reason you are allowed to look in this book is so that you will realize how shallow your book *Gnomes* is. Now that half the world has read that book and attached an exaggerated importance to it, things cannot be allowed to go on. It is time you grew up, and in the next few days you'll have the opportunity."

Our hearts beat faster from happiness. We had never been able to catch a glimpse of the Secret Book, which is kept in every gnome house. It appeared that the children did not even know where it was hidden in the house. Why hadn't this been able to take place somewhere in Holland? Mirko stalled our question by saying, "One of the reasons we let you come all the way to Lapland is this . . . the original Secret History Book. All other Secret Books have been taken from this one, transcribed in my house. When a gnome gets to be seventy-five years old and is registered by the local council, he comes here to do that. It takes him a couple of years. The

fact that we called you away at Christmas is due to this book having certain powers that you will soon witness, but the powers only work six days before and six days after Sunturn. That's why I couldn't wait for our guest, as you'll need a few days in which to study it."

Everyone was quiet. Elsa stared with glistening eyes and dilated pupils at the green radiance. We dared not touch the book.

"The reason I am allowed to look after such a valuable document," said Mirko, "is because we take it in turns, each for three hundred years. It might just as easily have been someone in Holland whose turn it was, but the one who looks after it has to keep it up to date." He

opened the book. The letters were green and appeared to be handwritten. By chance the book was open at the chapter called "Migration of Birds." On the page a primitive globe was drawn with crosshatching, dots, crosses, secret signs, and old Norwegian runic characters. But the longer you looked the higher the map seemed to rise from the page and the bigger it got; finally it began to revolve.

The green gave way to all sorts of other colors.

"Mention something you would like to know more about," said Mirko.

"Tern!" Immediately we could witness the migration of the Arctic tern,* east and west from both Americas,

and from Tierra del Fuego to Canada and back, a journey of tens of thousands of miles that takes them to their breeding grounds at least four times in a lifespan. Even the dreaded great skuas were illustrated which steal the fish caught by the tern on their long journey and devour their eggs in the breeding places.

It was a splendid sight. The globe was now floating high above the table and revolving slowly. Also revealed were the habitats of the sooty tern, black tern, whiskered tern, white wing, common tern, little tern, gull-billed tern, sandwich tern, and the rarer sorts of these intrepid birds. If you looked carefully it was just as if the white silhouettes of the birds were flying below you.

Mirko turned to the paleontology chapter under the section "Extinct Animals." At that instant the globe disappeared. "One difference between us," said Mirko, "is that we were here long before you—you only have the fossils from which to reconstruct the past! Would you like to see a mammoth?"

A terrifying hairy giant with enormous tusks rose from the page on the spot. It kept growing until it reached the ceiling and appeared to be alive. There was no communication between the beast and us. At one point Mirko put his hand clear through the animal.

* _Sterna macrura_

Yet it was so real that we imagined we could smell it, although it made no sounds at all.

Then Mirko showed us other prehistoric beasts. The appearance of Neanderthal man was staggering. He was busy scraping a hide with a stone; he also had no contact with us.

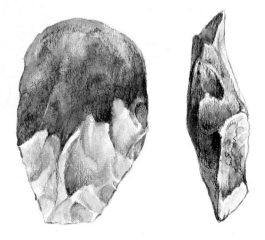

The gnomes know the whereabouts of cartloads of these stone-age tools.

We discovered that Napoleon had a gnome to keep him company on the island of Elba. Not only did they play chess together but they also took regular walks along the beach that did Napoleon no end of good, especially when he won at the contest of "who-can-spit-the-farthest."

Antonio Stradivari walked for miles through the mountains from Cremona, searching the forest for the right wood to make his incomparable violins.

The belly of a violin was made from even-grained boxwood (*Pinus silvestris*). The ribs, back, and neck were made from Bohemian ash. The varnish he used was a special composition, the recipe of which had been lost.

He preferred trees growing above an altitude of five thousand feet because their slow growth produced closely packed rings.

He often called on the gnomes for assistance. Apart from their material knowledge the gnomes were a particular help in that inaccessible countryside.

Eventually Mirko shut the book. Time had flown

and we had by no means seen everything. It was almost dawn when Elsa began to prepare the meal.

"What is in the small book?" we asked.

"This is the abbreviated version for the children," said Mirko. "We usually read from that one before they go to bed."

After dinner Mirko took the big book to the alcove and put it against the wall at the head of a large double bed. "Look in it as much as you like," he said soberly.

We undressed quickly and, having said goodnight to them all, got into bed and began to page through the book. We saw how the boomerang and the divining rod had been developed. The chapter on healing told us whatever we wanted to know. The information rose physically from the page. It was all there—up to and in-

cluding the latest Doppler apparatus for measuring the rate of the flow in the blood vessels.

Strangely enough, the pages stopped moving every now and then while the text continued, giving us the feeling of having fallen asleep over the newspaper.

We saw the tunnels that the gnomes had dug to the magma to convert warmth into energy, which is no easy task since the layer of stone that has to be bored through to reach the glowing sill is more than 1,000 miles deep. The sill crust is 850 miles deep, according to the gnomes, who also say that the earth's core consists of a solid mass with a diameter of 2,000 miles.

We learned all about the gnomes' methods of remote sensing and semantics. There was even an illustration of Noah's Ark!

The Flood took place at the end of the Stone Age, fourteen thousand years ago. Even gnomes could not ignore the Commandment: ". . . and of all living things, of all flesh, thou shalt bring one pair into the ark to be saved with thee, man and wife they shall be." They, like Noah, could take their children as extra guests.

During the disembarkation on Mount Ararat the gnome made himself useful by directing the animals to the various continents.

Here is one of the many pictures from the Secret Book
which we would call a puzzle picture —
intended more to keep gnomelets alert
rather than just for fun!

On the other hand, there are plates that depict quite innocent shapes which, especially in the half-dark, might seem grotesquely frightening.

These teach the gnomelets to differentiate between the harmless and the really dangerous ones (same for sounds).

Stream goddesses sometimes take on the form
of irresistibly beautiful women
who calmly inhabit icy-cold waters. ⟶

The man who looks at her immediately
forgets his wife and is doomed to
slavery for the rest of his life.

Gnomes are left alone
by these women.
—

or hawk eyes →

Some days the stream
goddesses like to complete
their toilet on
riverside rocks;
it is remarkable
how many time-
consuming jobs the
gnomes find to do
in the area.
←

"Roesalkas"
↓   are completely green
and some even have fish tails.
They are careless by nature and have no
idea of what they do to a man.
They get sick if their hair dries.

prehistoric reading board

← Pointed Cap writing from which cuneiform is derived is no longer used by gnomes.

(travelogue continued)

"May we see where the Secret Book is kept?" we asked Mirko after breakfast.

"Certainly," he answered brightly.

The lid of the hope chest lifted and we stepped inside. There was a large bright area below us that must have been situated under the living room. There were seven desks. . . .

The next morning we again took the book into the alcove. Apparently there was a lot more to it than we thought, and we had seen the previous day that this was only Part III.

One week passed.

One evening as we were finishing breakfast, the cuckoo clock struck twelve. According to our calculations it was January first.

We rubbed noses with Elsa and Mirko and wished them a happy New Year. "The storm is abating," said Mirko. "There will be no wind tomorrow but there is three feet of snow outside and it will freeze solid as soon as the wind stops. I am expecting our guest tomorrow toward evening. There are lots of trolls about and I've heard that an infamous band of ice trolls is roaming around and even tried to bring a snotgurgle to life. Our friend has to take all sorts of precautions!"

On the evening of January first we heard an urgent knocking at the copper door. Mirko answered it and who should come in . . . but a Siberian gnome! He was inches taller than us, and wore a garment of rough skins and a pointed fur cap with enormous earflaps. Below his penetrating eyes and red nose was a wild beard.

"Hello, Nicolas," said Mirko. "Welcome! You must have had a grueling journey."

The Siberian gave no reply. He turned around, unbuckled a heavy knapsack and, letting it slide off, pushed it with his foot against the wall. Then he threw his rough woolen mittens on it too. Only then did he turn to Mirko and say, stretching out a hamlike hand: "That bit of snow and wind? Don't make me laugh!"

He rubbed his nose with Elsa.

Facing us, he slowly examined us from head to toe while removing his garment, then walked off to the boot room to hang it up. When he returned Mirko said, "May I introduce you to our Dutch friends?"

The Siberian grunted and said, "Why? Aren't these the ones who knew so well that Siberians are all scoundrels and that my friend Kostja was a skin thief?"

We looked at each other. It was an awkward situation. Elsa and Mirko were embarrassed too. For the moment the arrival of the long-awaited guest was something of a disappointment. Mirko saved the day by saying, "That may be true, Nicolas Stepanowitsch, but there is such a thing as manners. Even if it were only toward Elsa and me. Now shake hands."

The Siberian sniffed, shrugged his shoulders, and begrudgingly offered us his hand. Then we sat down. Mirko went over to a cupboard and returned with a bottle and glasses. "How about a glass of mushroom gin?" he asked Nicolas. The guest gestured his assent.

We also were given brimming crystal glasses. When we had drunk to each other's health, a smile appeared on Nicolas's face. "How you always manage to make such delicious mushroom gin in Lapland is beyond me!"

He was right. It was an extraordinarily delicious drink In spite of our recent experience with him, we had

great respect for Nicolas. He was an enormous gnome and radiated an obstinacy that was probably well suited to his rugged existence in the never-ending taiga, a forest half the size of Europe. Perhaps this accounted for his not being the most pleasant gnome on earth.

He stretched his legs and appeared to doze off. He certainly must have had a tiring journey. No one spoke a word. Suddenly he opened his eyes, threw back his drink, and said, "A bear is trapped twenty-five miles from here. We must go immediately."

Before you knew it we were provided with saws, axes, ropes, knives, earmuffs, long underwear, and vests, which Mirko took from a cupboard in the passageway, and before long we were off on the skis. The gnomes' speed was killing. Mirko had to give us a caraway seed every quarter of an hour, otherwise we couldn't keep up.

The temperature was −30° F., but there was no wind. Forests, plains, and frozen marshes flew past. Nowhere did we sink into the snow, although it was many feet deep.

Finally, near a steep hill we saw a snow-sprinkled bear hanging motionless, jammed into a fork in a tree. He was scarcely breathing and his eyes were dull. The pressure on his ribs had probably cut off his breathing and he must have been half frozen. Mirko and Nicolas immediately began to hack at the outer side of the right branch.

When they had made a decent wedge, they climbed onto the other branch with a rope.

"You two go and stand under the bear," called Mirko. "When we let the ropes down, you must put them under the neck, foreleg, and back, and then throw the ends back up."

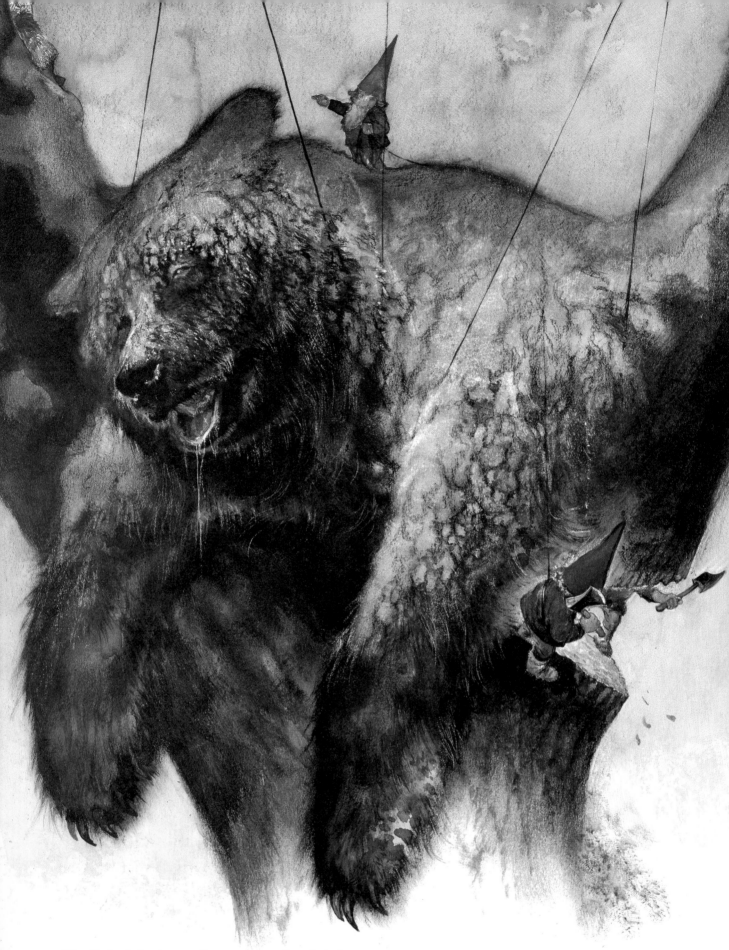

We climbed the tree so that we were directly below the nearly dead bear. The hairy, smelly, snow-covered body made an enormous impression on us. After three throws, the gnomes had all the rope ends and tied them to the trunk. Then they jumped down.

"Now saw on the inside of the fork," said Mirko. "Careful, because this branch will soon go crashing down."

The four of us sawed away. The tree began to crack and moved a bit. We sawed a few inches deeper. The cracking noise grew louder. The bear took one deep breath. Nicolas uttered an unintelligible bellow with lots of rolling r's.

And then, after sawing for another half an inch, the crown of the trunk gave way with an earsplitting crash and much falling snow, and disappeared into the depths of the steep slope. Now we saw how wise it had been to suspend the bear temporarily. He would otherwise have fallen fifteen feet, which would not have done any good for his frozen body. The bear would also have slid down the slope just like the fallen branch.

The gnomes climbed up again quickly, and we followed. The ropes were slowly relaxed. It succeeded! The bear must have weighed at least five hundred pounds, but we could hold him by sliding the ropes around the tree, which gave increased resistance. Apparently the ropes were as strong as iron.

At last the bear fell with a soft "plop" in the snow. When we were all down again and standing around him, Mirko took a bottle of arnica ointment out of his bag and began to rub the bear's bruised ribs with it. Meanwhile

Nicolas poured lobeline in the corners of the mouth to stimulate breathing. We rubbed snow into his limbs as hard as we could to get the blood flowing again. After half an hour the bear was visibly breathing more easily. He tried to get up but fell over each time. After a quarter of an hour he tried again. This time he remained standing, though he was swaying and completely drunk. His small eyes looked worried, but nevertheless grateful.

"How far is it to your lair?" asked Mirko.

The bear growled from somewhere deep in his throat.

"An hour! Can you make it?"

But the bear was already gone. Lumbering and sliding, he made his way from the slope until he finally disappeared into the dense wood.

"He'll make it," said Mirko reassuringly. "But he will have a couple of uncomfortable weeks. The storm must have awakened him from his hibernation."

At home the atmosphere was tense again. The trip to the bear had been a distraction from the menacing Nicolas and a welcome interruption of life under the earth, but once back again Nicolas made us feel uncomfortable.

He silently indulged in an enormous meal, interspersed with soft wine, and then stretched out in a hammock that had been slung for him across the living room and went to sleep with an ever-increasing snore.

The following night he told us that he had come to take us to Siberia and that there was no turning back. We had already apologized for our superficial handling of the first book but obviously that was not enough.

"A wonderful opportunity for your all-around improvement," said Mirko ambiguously. He must have known about this.

We tried to tell him that we thought this might be going overboard. We asked, "Who will make us big again?"

"We can do that in Siberia too," said Nicolas grimly.

"Why do we have to go to Siberia?"

"To realize why we called for you," said Mirko.

We could do no more. Besides, we felt it had nothing directly to do with our first book at all. Yet we gave it one more try: "Supposing you made us big right now so that we could go home?"

Mirko brushed aside this desperate attempt that would ordinarily have canceled out all intimacy between us and the gnomes. "I can do it," he said, "but I don't want to. You will understand everything later."

There was nothing more to do. All we could say was that we wanted to call home to report that we would be returning considerably later than we had anticipated, although of course no definite date had ever been mentioned. Mirko was more than willing and Nicolas couldn't care less.

Deep in the night we went to a village a few hours away from Mirko's house. All was quiet and still. Via an unused rat hole we got under a house and into the living room by squeezing through a crack in the floorboard. An antique telephone hung on the wall. It was ages before there was any reaction but eventually we got a crackly connection with Holland from a nocturnal voice in Helsinki.

We got our wives on the line; they were sleepy but pleased to hear from us, but less pleased when they heard we intended to stay longer. But we explained, while constantly juggling the telephone from ear to mouth, that we simply could not help it.

When we hung up, both rather moved, Mirko said, "You might not be looking forward to it, but it will be a marvelous experience, just you wait!"

At the time we did not agree with him whatsoever, but Mirko brushed aside all our objections, fished a lump of gold out of the depths of his pocket, and, laying it beside the telephone, said: "That ought to be enough."

Then we returned. No one spoke.

Two nights later we were to depart, but first Mirko

wanted to talk to us alone. Our thrill at the revelations in the Secret Book was tempered by the recent occurrences, partly because we had not managed to see the complete Book. We asked once but he silently shook his head. "That last part is what it's all about," said Mirko. "You are not ready yet to see the core. One or two things still have to happen to you."

He became very serious. "Don't think we behave without reason. This is what I mean: In the first place I'm not allowed to show you the complete Secret Book. Something has to happen first. Second, there wouldn't

be enough time. While transcribing the Secret Book, which consists of seven sections and which takes several years, each gnome undergoes a process of maturing that I cannot express in words."

"Why not?"

"Simply because you are not gnomes!" he said, more sternly than usual. It was all very mysterious and rather disappointing, but it was useless arguing any further. We were obviously in front of a door the gnomes did not want to open for us because "something has to happen first."

How and why the gnomes had command of such a vast number of abilities that the rest of the world would probably never have, must remain a mystery. They had from time immemorial continued the pattern of behavior of the animals of the field together with the serenely applied use of Reason. As a result of the perfect harmony with the world around them, they did not experience any neuroses despite that application of the highest Reason. They did not pursue power or personal gain but achieved the ideal collectivism. They put into practice the law of Nature that dictates that the survival of the species is more important than the individual, and at the same time mastered the paradox that consciousness brings with it—all this for thousands of years without strife, self-interest, violence, or pollution.

It seemed as though we had been brought to Lapland to be shown where it all was and that it all existed, but we had been weighed and found too wanting to be allowed to take a real part in it.

It was a hard lesson.

"But," resumed Mirko, sensing our dejection, "much will depend on you in the coming weeks. There is enough time. Wait patiently even if it is not always pleasant. Anyway, what you have seen in the Secret Book will stand you in good stead during the coming trials. Draw accurately. Nicolas is not as bad as he seems. He will be a great help. Farewell!"

END OF THE FIRST PART

THE JOURNEY TO SIBERIA

Gradually we began to realize how everything fit together. Mirko wanted us in Lapland to show us the Secret Book with its magic power during the midwinter period, but we would not be allowed to read it completely this time. That was the lesson of the western gnomes.

At the same time Mirko would invite a Siberian gnome, whose tribe was clearly antagonized by the remarks in our first book, to visit Lapland. This gnome would take us to Siberia. That was the lesson from the gnomes of the east. That was what we made of it.

It was decided that we would travel by a lemming-pulled troika. Our objective was the Yenisey River, about nineteen hundred miles ahead of us. We had dreaded the journey to Lapland but, compared with what we were about to undertake, that was child's play . . . and to think it was still winter and we were to be accompanied by a grumpy gnome! Furthermore, it was an enigma as to how the little lemmings could undertake such a gigantic journey.

Siberia! Three times the size of Russia proper. Temperatures as low as −65° F. The taiga, an all-but-endless pine forest with floods and swamps; the tundras; the permafrost. The colossal rivers like the Yenisey, the Ob, the Lena, all unexpectedly flowing north, making it impossible for the masses of melted ice in the south to flow away because the lower courses remain frozen, resulting in constant flooding. At last the moment had arrived. The troika stood in front of Elsa and Mirko's house with three strong East Russian lemmings ready to pull it.

Our luggage and book were on the sleigh, and we made our fond farewells. We did not, of course, want to give our real feelings away. We got in, and the troika shot off immediately.

We drew the heavy mammoth-hair rug over us. The animals found the way themselves. We gazed silently at the passing landscape. It was untouched and beautiful, even in the dark, but uncertainty gnawed at us and we wondered whether we would be able to stand the atrocious cold farther east. Nicolas did not utter a word and kept dozing off with intermittent snores. At regular intervals the lemmings stopped to rest and were given the grain Mirko had sent with us. The wind was mild and easterly.

The lemmings must have been dead tired by dawn, but they careened on, seemingly driven by something stronger than themselves. Sometimes they stopped to sniff the wind and then continued, barking, whining, and growling. Then, on a high plateau, they suddenly bolted. It was almost 10:00 A.M. The steep edge of the plateau came frighteningly near and we were afraid that we would be flung over the side, troika and all. Nicolas

sat up, drew his knife, and quick as lightning cut through the straps. While the lemmings disappeared before our eyes, over the side, the sleigh came to a halt exactly at the edge of the plateau. In the light of dawn we made out a brownish-white river far below us in the narrow valley. Soon we saw what it was: an endless stream of lemmings swarming eagerly southward. There must have been tens of thousands of them. We had hit upon the migration of the lemmings, which only happens once in five or eight years, and this one seemed exceptionally large.

Because of a number of favorable breeding years their numbers increase so rapidly that overpopulation results. Sometimes the females produce twelve offspring. The young of the first and second litter produce again within their first year, so that the increase via mathematical progression gets quite out of hand.

Normally they move from their winter abode in the mountains to the young spring grass of the lower reaches and return to the mountains in the autumn. In times of overpopulation the urge to migrate gets much stronger —away from the masses where sickness and famine lurk. The procession begins with tens but soon increases

to hundreds, thousands, and finally tens of thousands of lemmings.

Each animal has one goal: to get as far as possible, off to the horizon and even into glaciers. They cross rivers with ease, and even lakes, but finally they reach an ocean and, thinking this easy too, fling themselves in—sometimes from a great height—and drown en masse.

Needless to say, every animal or fish of prey helps to decimate the helpless columns.

It is touching to witness the courage of the little rodents: even against fox and wolf they adopt an aggressive attitude, balancing on their hind legs with backward-bent head.

Far below we saw our lemmings being admitted into the stream of animals. We lowered the troika over the edge of the plateau and hid it in the cleft of a rock. We took our luggage out and silently stared at Nicolas. That was the moment we heard the first friendly word from him: "Well done! No nagging about going back now?"

We started off for a forest on the far side of the valley and had to pass through the lemming column. For some reason we were not run over. Nicolas said, "They nearly all die. But it has been like that for centuries." He appeared to be less remote. It seemed as though his gruff manner was a bit put on. Soon we smelled a fox in the forest. Nicolas whistled hard on his fingers and in no time a penetratingly smelly white fox was standing before us. Nicolas whispered something in his ear. The fox agreed hesitatingly. "He will take us a good way east," said Nicolas, "although the rascal would rather go with the lemmings."

We jumped onto the back of the fox and held on tight to the deep, thick fur undercoat. We felt the rhythmical contracting and relaxing of the muscles under the supple skin during the fox's undulating gallop. The wind whistled through our hair.

Hours later Nicolas shouted "Stop!" Once we climbed down he sent the fox back on his own tracks. "That is to fool the trappers. Also I had to have him out of the way in connection with our accommodation tonight!"

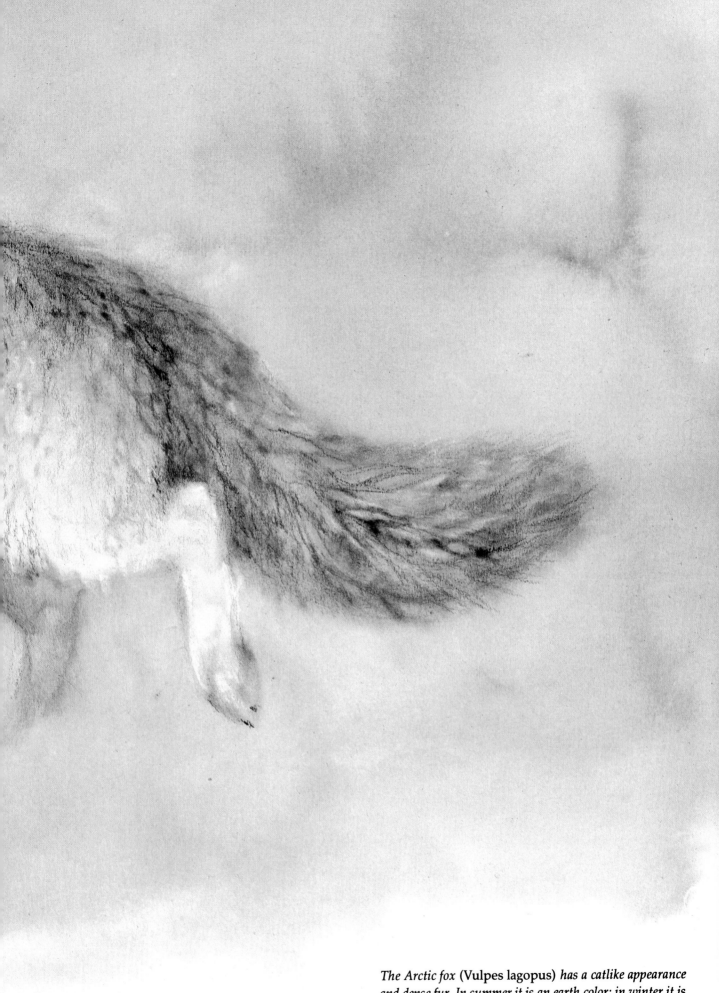

The Arctic fox (Vulpes lagopus) has a catlike appearance and dense fur. In summer it is an earth color; in winter it is as white as snow. One variation is the blue fox.

We skied on a heathery plain interspersed with birch trees to an embankment with bushes, deep under snow. When Nicolas pushed aside a few branches, the entrance to a den was visible. He went in and spoke to someone far inside. Then he came back and said: "It's fine. We can stay here today. I shall introduce you to our host, a blackcock!"

We stuck the ends of our skis in the snow and went in. The blackcock looked at us fearlessly. He lifted one wing and we made ourselves comfortable against his warm body; then he draped his wing gently over us. We could feel his breathing and heartbeat but we were so tired that we soon fell asleep.

When we awoke it must have been evening. After our rest in the delicious feather bed we began to discuss the lemmings. Nicolas was nowhere as friendly as he had been that morning, but he did join in. "There are

Blackcocks making curving passages in the snow about three feet long. At the end there is a sitting room. Because of their high body temperature, a small air hole forms on the top of their head. Sometimes they spend an entire day in this den when their crop is full of heather and birch buds.

thousands of natural laws," he said, "against which we can do nothing. If an animal is in danger we are prepared to help him, as with the bear. But if it is a law of nature we can do nothing about it. The balance restores itself though it may seem cruel. One animal eats the other, but they never exterminate each other—only you do that. A lynx kills a roe deer for food. The sick, weak, and old are removed. That is not cruel, it is lack of compassion, which makes all the difference. It always makes sense. Only degenerate beings kill for nothing."

As we stood outside the den, the starry heavens stretched mightily above us. We put on our skis to explore the surrounding countryside. In some places the snow had been pushed aside and the heather below had been eaten. There were hollows smelling of animals just as deep in the snow as we had been. "Moose," mumbled Nicolas.

It was midnight by the time we returned to the den

of the blackcock. Instructed by Nicolas, we dug a square in the ground under the snow, lined it with flat stones, and lit a good fire. On leaving to find edible plants, he said: "Use the time to work on your book. I'll be back in a couple of hours."

When he returned with arms full of plants we made an earth oven.

Flat stones are placed in a square hole in the ground (don't use river stones—they explode!). A good fire can be kept burning for two hours on these stones. The glowing ashes are then spread out. Now the leathery leaves of the rock tripe (Umbilicaria) are spread on the stones. Over them goes a thick layer of the finer branches of reindeer moss (Cladonia rangiferina), with wild onion bulbs (Allium) and rose hips (Rosa) on top. The next layer is more rock tripe, and then the whole thing is covered with a layer of earth.

Everything was cooked in an hour and the top layer of earth removed to reveal a steaming mass of vegetables before us. We consumed them at our leisure during the night.

Nicolas was grumpy but he poured us a generous acorn cup of fruit wine that he somehow had with him in spite of having left the troika behind. We were slowly beginning to appreciate him. "How could you find all those plants in the snow?" we asked.

"Reindeer moss grows everywhere. Wild onions are found below places where water collects. Those you can find without a divining rod, in folds of the ground. Rose hips hang above the snow, and can be found under it too, though they are somewhat damaged by the frost; nevertheless here they are."

Mother Earth was once more a tangible thing. You just had to have the feel for it.

To avoid getting scurvy in the long Arctic winters when there are no green vegetables available, gnomes boil fir branches in water. The liquid contains just enough vitamin C to prevent the feared disease. As a result of lack of vitamin C hemorrhages occur in the muscles, under the periosteum of the long bones, and in the gums. If vitamin C is not administered in time, an extremely painful death follows. Another method is to drink the blood of a wolf or a dog, as these animals manufacture their own vitamin C. It is simpler to let the blood from the bast antlers of a reindeer, for it won't cause the animal to die. The bast antlers grow in early spring when the vitamin C content of the food is the lowest.

Toward morning, our feathered host came into the open. His colors were a feast for the eye, but his eyes were gloomy.

"He is in trouble," said Nicolas. "There is a capercaillie in the vicinity that not only disrupts all caper marriages, but also interferes with the ritual dance of the blackcocks. I think I shall have to do something about it."

Reindeer moss (Cladonia rangiferina)

"Can you?" we asked.

He frowned, whistled thoughtfully, and said, "Oh, very well then. I shall make an admission: I am a justice of the peace and I have to make decisions in all sorts of disputes. I am absolutely bound to appear wherever and whenever a complaint arises. I have set the session for seven o'clock tonight. First, let's get some sleep. Our host is too agitated to put us up now so we shall have to find another."

One heath farther we found a gray hen in the room. It was a sweet animal that sheltered us for the day as though we were her three chickens to be kept warm. We were so tired that we fell asleep immediately.

We awoke quite refreshed and, as we had the day before, chatted a bit; it was one of the gossips that we shall not forget for the rest of our lives. "Do you know why wild nature trails* always throw off light?" asked Nicolas. "It's because animals react to secret signs that elude people—for example, beams, magnetic waves,

and horizon changes. Perhaps humans were once able to perceive these things, but not anymore. A sled dog like the husky realizes from the color of the snow, a change of echo, a certain smell, an unusual tremor in the ice, and from great experience and instinct that a hidden fissure in the ice lays snow-covered in front of him, and he stops. Just try to copy that!"

We bid the gray hen adieu. She appeared grateful. Obviously she was honored and we had flattered her maternal feelings.

Meanwhile we were intrigued by the forthcoming court case. We skied after Nicolas to a wood on the horizon. There was already a snow-cleared area under the trees. In the middle was a round rock. Out of his suitcase Nicolas took a black gown with long white bands. Capercaillies were standing nearby and beyond them were some shy willow grouse and other onlookers.

* *A nature trail is a path frequented by wild animals.*

When Nicolas, adorned in his long toga, had taken his place on the stone, we heard the case of the blackcock, who was applauded by a whole group of capercaillies that had streamed in from all sides. Then came several capercaillie witnesses. It appeared that the capercaillie in question had gone much too far and could not leave the chickens alone. When the capercaillie gave his testimony it seemed to us that his defense was weak. Quite honestly, we did not think he was all there. We gained even more respect for Nicolas after hearing his questioning, which was conducted without any hurry. His command of the situation, his clear summing up, and especially his humor impressed us deeply. Secretly we agreed that he was the last person we would like to face if we had done something wrong.

When Nicolas had considered all the facts, he passed judgment. He denied the capercaillie, on penalty of having his wings clipped, the right to more than one hen per season and commanded him to abstain from all other disturbing activities, a decision that was received with loud applause from the audience. Thus the session was closed as there were no further complaints.

"Does he abide by your verdict?" we asked Nicolas.

"He better," he said severely. "I have my animal auxiliaries for this."

He changed into his normal clothes and we left. It was a cold and still Arctic night but we felt cozy. The snow squeaked softly under our skis and the clean, pure air filled our lungs. Hidden behind that gruff exterior Nicolas had a strong sense of justice and a good heart.

We realized that it was no accident that we had been sent to Siberia with this gnome but decided to ask him about it later anyway.

During a moment's pause we asked, "Do you get many such requests?"

"It never stops," he said. "The stream of complaints is endless. There are quarrels between animals, plants, stones, and even rivers about ownership, damage, theft, and dishonesty. Three of us control the area from Lapland as far as the Yenisey River, but we could use one more. I prefer to administer justice from a mushroom but with the snow of course there are none. My father and grandfather were both justices of the peace. We acquire the knowledge from each other, then we spend a couple of years at court to learn the fine points. My grandfather introduced the ruling that the badger and the fox could easily live together under one roof. The ruling that a roebuck, or for that matter any male animal, could chase an intruder from his territory up to and even a little be-yond the boundary—but that aggression had to stop there—was introduced much earlier. This we enforce to the letter. My grandfather witnessed the case of the wolf and the fox: A wolf and a fox, both starving, saw a mare with her foal in a field. The fox sent the wolf to ask the mare if she would sell her foal, while he himself waited behind the fence. 'Certainly,' she said. 'Only I have completely forgotten the price. Would you look for yourself, Mr. Wolf? It is written under my right back hoof.' She lifted her hind leg for the wolf to see and gave him such a mighty kick that he lay unconscious for hours. The wolf then lodged a complaint against the fox for his trickery, and my grandfather had to deal with it. The wolf got no compensation or redress because he had willingly gone to the mare and should have been craftier, although my grandfather did give the fox a serious warning not to play such dirty tricks again."

While we were skiing along he continued: "Then there are the constantly recurring damage claims: trees complaining that rabbits gnaw on their roots or grub

them up; morning glories that strangle alders and willows; aggressive armies of ants that attack and devour everything in their path. There are complaints from the insect world about the red forest ants,* and so on. Last year a herd of red deer caused a rockslide that dammed a river. An area full of ground nesters was flooded just at breeding time. Luckily it was early spring so there was still time to build new nests. I sentenced each deer to protect three nests against predators and other menaces. The deer had to do so till the chickens were old enough to accompany their mothers. Naturally we got protests about this from foxes, martens, hedgehogs, crows, and

* A red forest ant colony consists of about one million inhabitants and consumes one hundred thousand insects per day from the surrounding forest.

magpies, but I ignored them. I deal regularly with bears that have stolen honey from a beehive. The bees approach me for damages because they can't do anything to the bears themselves. Bears are immune to bee stings except in the eye corners and the lips, but there he just wipes them away. Moreover, once it has stung a bee dies whereas a wasp doesn't. Above all, honey is the bees' foodstore for the winter. Naturally I'm talking about wild bees. They exist too, you know.

"The bear usually starts off with a denial, but in the face of twenty thousand witnesses he hasn't a leg to stand on. The only punishment I could impose would indeed be that the bear return the honey or at least sugar to the hive, but that is not easy in the wild. Usually such a bear gets away with a reprimand but I'm afraid I don't have many friends left among the bees."

The story of
    Little Red Riding Hood and
    the wolf can't be true.
    Who would call a girl
    Red Riding Hood
    (and how could she appear
     in one piece out of a wolf's
     stomach), just to mention
     a few discrepancies?

It's more likely that a
wolf with rabies ate a
she-gnome (with a pointed red cap)
by mistake.

Punch and Judy were
originally gnomes.
It happened like this:
Since olden days the gnomes,
as born actors, have given
their own shows at fairs
and annual markets,

and they have given
any money collected
to the poor.

Their wit and talent always stole
the show and caused professional
jealousy among bear owners, players,
quacks, fire-eaters, and magicians. That's why they
were expelled from their place in society in the
sixteenth and seventeenth centuries.

Naturally crafty chaps had long realized there was money to be made with this sort of entertainment.

They made hand puppets to imitate gnomes, thereby fooling simple people.

Over the years the gnomes' beard became the protruding chin of Punch and the pointed cap tilted forward.

Later, stupid tumbling toys and the insulting gnome pull toy were invented.

And the boring garden gnome

It might only be used by an old dog

to lift his leg on...

After Nicolas told us all this, we smelled a moose in the dense wood. In front of us we discovered a track; indeed it was difficult not to fall head over heels in the deep prints, and we had to bypass dung heaps as tall as we were.

The hoof mark of a bull moose is 4–6 inches long and 4–5 inches wide. The excrement is nearly as high as a gnome.

Moose and, to a lesser extent, Iceland ponies have an arched nose they use as a snowplow to collect food. The nostrils are placed fairly far back so that no snow can get in.

Finally we heard sniffing in front of us. We came across two bulls, one young and the other old. The older bull had lost his antlers. They towered above us with their enormous heads bowed to the ground. Nicolas spoke to them. It seemed less difficult than it was with the fox. "The older bull has just shed his antlers," our guide said. "That makes a difference of forty pounds. He will take us part of the way."

An hour later we were storming through field and forest at a great height with the wind whistling in our ears. The young moose had come along too. The older one, upon whose head we sat, was careful to see that we were not whisked off by passing branches. Their long-legged trot could evidently be kept up for hours. They stopped toward morning, promising to return later to take us a little farther. After they left, Nicolas explained: "Moose do not have a permanent home. They roam. They travel hundreds of miles in the mating season."

While we were searching for a blackcock's hole we noticed a straight line of small trees. "Those were planted by gnomes," Nicolas said, "to enable them to cross from one hiding place to another without being seen."

Within a quarter of an hour we had found a blackcock's spoor, and after a number of U-turns, doubling back, circles, and other peculiar maneuvers, it ended at a hole.

We followed the same procedure as we had before.

While Nicolas was away looking for food we kept warm by the earth oven and worked on the book, which had been wrapped and placed at the bottom of our knapsack. A magic spell seemed to flow from it just by holding it, and while leafing through the entries we had made, we were conscious of all sorts of intangible things around us.

After supper we once again crept "under wing" and slept soundly till evening. We felt we were one with life on earth.

Our appreciation of each other increased as it is often apt to do when people are thrown together. That evening, upon waking under the wing, Nicolas even muttered, "So, old chaps, slept well?"

Our conversation touched on plant life. "Naturally a plant registers what goes on around him or her," said

Nicolas. "It has a primeval perceptive faculty that existed among living cells long before the five senses. It is not bound by time or space. Something happens of which one is simply part. A tree experiences being chopped down as a human would experience being led to the gallows. It is odd that you people have such a considerable knowledge of the workings of the heart and brain, aided only by weak electric currents, and yet you are deaf to these plant signals!"

The moose returned the following evening. The east wind had become a strong west wind. Nicolas rubbed his hands together as he looked at the sky and mumbled, "We can soon travel faster!"

"Do you mean by bird?"

"Just wait patiently!" he said mysteriously.

By morning the moose had done forty miles. We alighted, thanked them, and sent them back. We were on a wooded slope.

In the moonlight we noticed a cave dug into the side of the hill. Nicolas shouted a few unintelligible words as we drew near, whereupon there was a sound of yawning and shuffling. To our horror, a broad-shouldered troll appeared. Nicolas gestured to us reassuringly and said, "So, Cork. Everything all right?"

For sheer joy at seeing Nicolas, the troll began to jump up and down with his flailing flat feet. "Shake hands with my friends," commanded Nicolas.

Cork wiped his hands under his armpits and offered us a greasy, bristly troll hand. "Is everything ready?" Nicolas asked.

"Quite so. A balloon," said Nicolas. "Made from the bladder of a mammoth. It contains fifty-three cubic feet of natural gas."

"A mammoth bladder?"

"Yes. There are still plenty of mammoths to be found in the permafrost. It takes one slash in the abdomen, bladder out, abdomen closed. Then wash, salt, and dry the bladder. It is then so elastic it can be blown up to many times its original size."

"And the gas?"

"Our good friend Cork gets that out of the ground. He has improved so much that he can say twelve words without one mistake. He is paid in food and gold to have a balloon ready here at all times. Between here and the Yenisey River we have three such trolls. This is Cork I. We have Cork II, Cork III, and finally Crown Cork; one every five hundred miles."

Cork grinned broadly at these words. Bellows hung on the wall. There were balloon baskets of woven reed, a couple of nets, and an empty reserve balloon.

"Cork can mend nets and repair baskets now," said Nicolas. "He even is house-trained. It has taken years."

"Where does the gas come from?"

"Deep in the ground. It is a slow process, bellow by bellow, but Cork has oceans of time. There are still ancient reserves stored up by the gnomes."

"Tonight we take off, Cork," Nicolas said to the obediently listening troll with arms hanging at his sides. "See that everything is in order and get a blanket for us."

The blanket Cork took from a wall cupboard smelled fresh, as if it had been plunged into a mountain stream.

Nicolas took hard-baked biscuits and nuts from another cupboard and made tea on a primitive stove. He slept on the blanket after supper but we got caught up in our book, which we managed to work on without getting cold fingers. After three hours we too went to sleep; Nicolas was snoring beside us. Cork lay in a corner on a bed of fir branches. The balloon cast huge shadows on the ceiling. It was eerie.

The troll nodded emphatically and we entered a short passageway leading to a large space where a night-light was glowing and, of all things, a balloon was hanging from the ceiling. We stared incredulously.

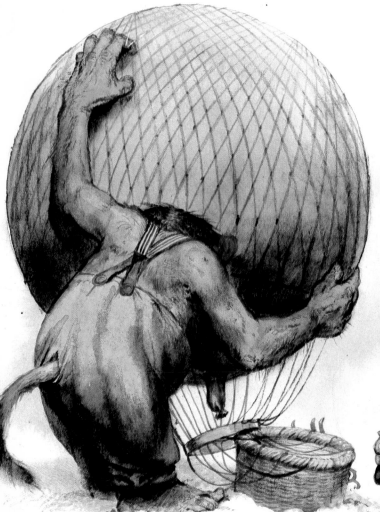

When we awoke, Nicolas had three plates of steaming porridge ready that he had sprinkled liberally with sugar. The balloon had disappeared and there was a sound outside of falling gravel.

"Cork puts pebbles in the basket as ballast," said Nicolas. "We will leave as soon as we have eaten."

When we went out, the balloon looked even bigger. "Cork has put in a bit more gas," said Nicolas. "When it is completely full it won't fit through the passageway. It's now twelve and a half times lighter than air."

In one hand Cork held a rope and with the other he was throwing pebbles into the basket, which also contained a blanket.

The net was neatly draped over the balloon and attached to the basket by the string ends. Nicolas threw in a bag of nuts and dried mushrooms and said, "Well done, Cork. I'm satisfied."

We stepped in while Cork held on to the balloon. As he eased off the ropes, the balloon rose ten feet, and we jumped up and down and stamped as directed by Nicolas, just like experienced balloonists.

"Is everything ready?" asked Nicolas, a bit out of breath from stamping. "Here we go then! Let go, Cork!"

A troll that walks into a gnome trap is set free after a few days (the days are counted by undoing one knot per day from a knotted rope). Sometimes the troll must spend a few extra days on a rock in the middle of a river . . . a troll cannot swim and is therefore terrified of water. Most trolls return to the forest swearing and cursing without improving a bit, but it does sometimes happen that a troll repents. If his intelligence seems any higher than other trolls', he is trained as a balloon-ready holder. The gnomes make the balloon, rigging, and basket, but the troll has to keep it ready for use filled with gas.

On the following pages are various traps used to overpower trolls.

Not out of hate but because of the endless teasing and senseless destructiveness of the troll, the gnome builds troll traps, for which he is here seen carving the "decoys" (decoy gnomes).

The troll doesn't understand wood-carving (his imagination doesn't stretch that far) but can only discern things he can pester, although anyone with sense would see that a wooden gnome strung up by his pointed hat isn't real.

Once in the trap, the troll pulls the door closed behind him and remains there trotting in an endless circle — for lack of any constructive thinking — until he is freed by the gnome.

Even the simplest trap principle is a sure success!

Whether a flower, mushroom, or a brood of eggs
is concerned — no matter what —
the troll rushes at it
with but one thought
in mind:

SQUASH IT!

SQUASH IT!

The FIST-PUNISHER is based on this squasher
principle:

it packs a hefty punch,
and even when the axle is
frozen stiff in icy
weather the sharpened
wooden cap comes
into its own.

There are many variations on a theme: decoy gnome and charging idiot.

The punishment element speaks for itself!

In spite of everything, the gnome still shows compassion for the troll!

The so-called
WRIST-TRAP
is made in an
old woodpecker's hole. →

No sooner does the red
pointed hat inside
catch the eye of our
dirty friend

then, grab-bang,
the wrist goes
in
↓

and the
silence of
the
forest
is rudely broken by
screams and curses.

Anything colorful
that dares to
appear has
to be broken.

As soon as the infant trolls are born they start kicking
around blindly. Only the meanest kicker remains alive,
sometimes one out of a nest of five.
The yelping victims do not even cause the mother to turn around.
Senseless destruction of a bird is obviously more interesting.

gnomes protect their homes adequately against retaliation
by the trolls by making a signpost with
the arrow pointing the wrong way.
——
Friends and trusted visitors just know
they have to go the other way.

(travelogue continued)

The balloon surged up about a hundred feet and was caught by the wind. Below us the forest passed by quickly while the balloon continued to rise. It was probably terribly cold outside but it didn't worry us. After a while we didn't notice the wind either, because we were traveling just as fast. The air was still. Nicolas held a cord connected to a valve that would let gas out of the balloon when we wanted to descend.

"My guess is that the wind is about twenty-two miles per hour," he said. "If we keep on like this we will reach Cork II in twenty-four hours. Anything could happen . . . the wind could slow or change course!"

Everything was going according to plan. We kept pace with the clouds above us, flying at a height of about three hundred and fifty feet. At one point we had to clear a high hill, which necessitated throwing a couple of handfuls of pebbles overboard. We saw a herd of deer now and then and a solitary bear. Once trolls pelted stones at us but there was no danger of our being hit.

The endless forest was broken here and there by cultivated fields or a village, but no one saw us and we floated thirteen hundred feet high without interference because, Nicolas said, that was the best height to avoid opposing air currents.

It snowed toward morning and the balloon soon had

a cap of snow, so we once again had to unload some stones. "We shall have to fly on during the day," said Nicolas. "Luckily the area between the rivers Onega and Severnay is thinly populated." We cracked some nuts and ate dried mushrooms in fruit wine. It was a mystery to us where Nicolas got all that drink.

Dusk fell and we again drifted into the night.

Toward morning we saw a reddish glow on the eastern horizon. "The industrial zone of Syktyvkar," said our guide. "We have to go beyond it. There is an airport. Let's hope they don't spot us."

Fortunately the balloon was too small to be detected by their radar. Or they thought it was a child's balloon.

Or the air-controllers were napping. In any event we glided over without any trouble, although every now and then the air was full of suffocating smoke and we saw the fiery glow of the ovens directly below us.

There was still a strong wind as the clouds began to break. Nicolas looked at the stars and grunted contentedly. He pulled on the gas-outlet string and there was a hiss. The earth approached slowly. As the treetops sped past increasingly nearer, Nicolas made us jettison all the stones so that we rose somewhat. He let out more gas above a deep river valley and the balloon descended at an oblique angle to the frozen river behind the shelter of the hill.

Once down we stretched our stiff legs and wandered about a bit. Then we put on skis and went off. Within half an hour we reached a small house built on a sawed-off fir trunk with a ladder leaning against it. A small troll who appeared more intelligent than Cork I appeared in the doorway. He looked unhappy.

"Is everything all right?" Nicolas asked.

"No," said the troll. "Old comrades been here."

"What is broken?"

"Everything. Leak in balloon. Net torn. Basket stolen. Food eaten. Me hit and kicked!"

We climbed up and examined the damage. Cork II lifted up a balloon full of holes.

Nicolas walked around grunting and furiously kicked the pieces of ruined net in the air. "They will pay for this!" he said. "Who were they?"

The balloon troll on duty has a weather vane to indicate which way the wind is blowing and thus which way the balloon will go. In addition, the weather vane provides company for the troll, and gives him the happy feeling that a friend is there, helping him day and night, to whom he can wave and speak, and whom he has to protect against other trolls.

"Stamp, Gnash, and Fist. Far away now!"

"I'll get them," said Nicolas. "Will you fetch our balloon? It is a little way upstream, on this side."

Cork II disappeared with the speed of a beast of prey.

Nicolas said, "We must use our own balloon again. But filling it with gas takes a couple of days."

We had nuts and mushrooms for one more meal and then went to sleep. Meanwhile Cork had returned with the balloon and basket, but had left again by the time we awoke. "He is fetching gas," said Nicolas, "from a deep cleft in the earth where we have been getting it for centuries."

While Nicolas was away looking for vegetables, Cork appeared periodically with bellows of gas. As soon as Nicolas returned we made another earth oven. Then we climbed up into the house and spent half the night talking about the climate behind the Urals, and other things. We drew as much as we could in the book and fell asleep toward morning. Cork shuffled back and forth outside. He had to be careful of the daylight, as direct sun rays turn a troll to stone.

We were awakened by Cork's proud announcement at the top of the ladder: "Balloon ready!" It was pitch black outside. The balloon was hanging high up in the air. Cork gave Nicolas a huge sack. He looked in it and said, "Well, what do you know—hazelnuts! Where did you find these?"

"Fetched them," said Cork. "From far! For Nicolas."

"Good troll," said Nicolas with great appreciation. "You will get an honorable mention."

After this we skied away to collect reindeer moss, and Nicolas showed us how to find it in the snow. We returned an hour and a half later. Nicolas said to Cork once more: "I am really very satisfied. You have done exceptionally well," whereupon Cork turned scarlet and wiped his nose on his upper right arm.

We were soon rising above the trees in our basket. The wind blew the balloon above us obliquely eastward and before long we were swinging calmly in a moderate breeze about eight hundred feet above the endless waves of forest landscape.

We did one hundred twenty-five miles at the beginning of the evening, until the wind increased our speed; it got colder. The next sixty miles went one and a half times as fast. The icy air filled our eyes, and icicles formed on our mouths and noses. Nicolas looked anxiously at the sky. "We are getting into a storm," he said, "but I want to take advantage of our speed for as long as possible." Squalls tossed the basket and balloon backward and forward. Our speed rose alarmingly. Nicolas made us jettison stones in the belief that the squalls would be less severe at a higher altitude, which luckily proved to be correct.

The landscape below flew by at a tremendous speed as the storm increased in strength. We had to scream to make ourselves heard and felt terribly uncomfortable, but we made enormous progress. Nicolas remained calm.

Toward morning the sky lightened to a yellow-gray. It was abominably cold, we were exhausted, and the storm had increased to a hurricane. Finally Nicolas shouted, "The wind is veering to the south. We must go down or we will be blown off course."

We sighed with relief. To be safely on the ground among solid trees or in a cave seemed like it would be heaven after this terrifying storm. But when Nicolas pulled the rope to let the gas escape, nothing happened. The valve was stuck! We all pulled on the rope to no avail. The balloon was lifted now by the hurricane and in fits and starts we went higher and higher. Sometimes the hurricane seemed to be aiming direct blows at us. Nicolas climbed in the rigging. When he was back in the basket he shouted, "The valve is frozen shut with ice. Nothing can be done about it. We'll just have to make the best of it!"

The next twelve hours passed in a stupor. Dawn broke, eclipsed by heavy, dark clouds. One moment there was sleet, then snow. There were no longer forests below us; plains stretched as far as the eye could see. We must have been blown far to the north. Our limbs were

stiff and our only solace was from the drink and nuts provided by Cork II. We were exhausted from the constant swinging of the basket, to say nothing of our anxiety about the whole ordeal. We must have done six hundred miles. We were heading toward the Arctic Ocean when the hurricane lost some of its fury. Then, however, the ominous black clouds erupted—snow first, then hail. (Remember, a hailstone to a gnome is as big as his foot!) Most of the hailstones hit the balloon but some struck us like bricks. Above us sledgehammer blows rained on the balloon. Suddenly Nicolas pushed up his earflaps. We heard hissing. He pointed upward and shouted, "The balloon is leaking!"

The swollen balloon had not been able to withstand the drumming blows of the hailstones. We began to de-scend and quickly plunged at an angle to the ground that we had been longing for during the last hours. It would be a hard landing. We hit the ground in a cloud of snow and the basket bounced. Finally, after being hurled across the snowy plain, the balloon came to a standstill near the banks of the frozen Arctic Ocean. The hailstorm had stopped. We got out, stiff and numb. Nicolas said, "We can't stay here. We must get to the snow peaks on the other side, where we can build an igloo or perhaps find a polar bear's den. Right now I need to find mud. There must be soil so near the bank." He cut a square of ice loose. "We will tie that behind the basket," he said. "Then we will stay on course." We helped him enlarge the hole in the ice until we dug through to the earth, about one and a half feet deep.

Just as the Eskimos do with the underside of their sleighs, he rubbed the bottom of our skis with mud, let it freeze, wet it again, and then smoothed it with his knife to get a glossy surface. We then tied the skis side by side under the basket while Nicolas attached the ice block. We folded the balloon, stepped in the basket, and gave the whole thing a push with the ski poles till it was swept forward by the wind. We could maneuver by steering the ice block to the left or right. For the moment we thought the worst had passed.

The basket slid effortlessly over the vast expanse of ice, which was in itself a pleasant feeling, though we couldn't help wondering how we were ever going to get back to Holland. Three hours later, when we finally reached a high cliff of ice on the other side of the frozen estuary, we could find no trace of a polar bear. "We'll have to build an igloo," Nicolas said.

Building an igloo: wedge-shaped blocks are cut from the ice with a snow saw. Rings of ice blocks are placed in a spiral until the top of the round building is completed. The builder stands inside. The final piece at the center top is a block of ice with an air hole in it. When the builder is finished he hacks a low passage to the outside and makes a roof over it. A well-built igloo never collapses and is only rendered stronger by a slight sagging. All openings are closed off by an extra layer of snow.

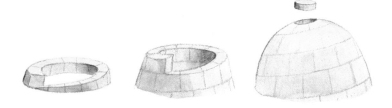

When the igloo was ready we pulled the balloon inside. There was plenty of room to sleep on it and we turned up the edges as a sort of blanket. Without fuel for a fire we had to eat the reindeer moss raw. Our problems dominated our thoughts. We were sheltered for the moment but this situation could not go on indefinitely. Nicolas was buried in thought. At last he said: "Let's sleep first. After that I'll leave to find help—alone!"

"What about us?" we asked. "Must we stay here alone?"

"You are safe here. The snow will quench your thirst—let it melt slowly in your mouth. There are still some nuts and reindeer moss. I'll be back in three or four days—I can go faster on my own. I'll leave some brandy."

"What about you?"

He slapped his stomach with his broad hand and laughed, "I can easily go for days on snow and nuts!"

We watched sadly as he left at noon, but realized that his iron constitution was well suited for feats of endurance. The loneliness of the igloo became unbearable after a few hours. We needed exercise and the best thing to do was to get out and ski. As long as we kept sight of the ice cliff, it was practically impossible to get lost. There was no wind and because we were on the move we were able to keep fairly warm in spite of our insufficient clothing. The landscape was monotonous. We felt hungry and ate a nut. Would we be able to see the renowned northern lights? They were reputed to be soft green and violet; for the present we saw nothing. We were amazed at the distance even the slightest sound traveled.

Suddenly we noticed two specks ahead of us on the ice, one large and one small. As we approached we discovered that they were seals, a mother with her pup; they had crept onto the ice from their breathing hole. Perhaps we could cadge a fish from them! Gnomes might be vegetarians but that didn't have to apply to us. And who could say when Nicolas would return? We considered fish a welcome complement to our meager menu.

The seals were not frightened of us—we must have been gnome enough—they just gazed at us with bulging eyes. The pup was a darling. When we asked the mother if she would catch us a fish she said nothing but stared over our heads into the distance. Obviously she could not quite place a request like this from a gnome. We would have to catch one for ourselves. At least she didn't object to our using her hole for this.

We returned to the hole two hours later, having made a hook from the pin in a belt buckle and a line from string on the balloon. We chewed up a hazelnut, put the resulting concoction on the hook, and froze it. We then placed it gingerly in the hole. There was no trace of the seals. Since we didn't have a float we had to keep pulling up the line at the slightest movement. Nothing was happening—the fish were either asleep or not at home. Sometimes the bait disintegrated in the water. We sat next to the hole for hours, getting unbearably cold. Now and then the seals would surface in our hole or the neighboring hole, which naturally scared the fish away.

Hours and hours passed without any luck until at last there was a flailing resistance in the depths. Thrilled, we both clung to the line. It must be a giant fish. We let him tire before pulling him in, afraid that he would escape from the slippery makeshift hook. We succeeded in getting him onto the ice: a flounder seven inches long! Food for days. We slapped each other proudly on the back. We killed the flounder immediately to save its suf-

fering unnecessarily and went back to the igloo, dragging the fish behind us on the line. It got misty but we could keep the cliff in view.

At one point we happened to look behind us and froze with fright. An enormous monster was following us. It was the size of an elephant but had a long tail and a huge panting mouth full of teeth. It appeared to be close behind us, and we fully expected it to charge at any moment. Blind with fear we made for the protection of the cliff; perhaps we could find a place to hide. The monster followed us with huge leaps. In fact it should already have been upon us. We dropped the fish and crept behind a ledge in the cliff. A wedge of ice fell with a loud

thud behind us; at that moment the monster vanished. We looked across the ice plain and saw an Arctic fox approaching in the distance. He was following the scent of the fish with his nose to the ice. We climbed down quickly and waited by the flounder for the fox to reach us. He lifted his head, put his nose in the air to get our scent, and looked disbelievingly from the fish to us and back, but he didn't take the fish.

We stood face to face like this for some time. Eventually he turned and trotted off and we pulled our forthcoming meal to the igloo. We lashed the fish under the upturned balloon basket behind the igloo. Then we went inside, ate half a nut each, and fell into a deep sleep.

It was evening when we awoke and we crawled to the outside. The flounder had not been touched. Apparently there were no more foxes or polar bears in the vicinity. We each hacked off a generous piece from the solidly frozen fish and took them inside. Frozen raw flounder turned out to be a delicacy. We ate copious amounts of it, swilling it down with brandy, and peacefully fell asleep again. The next day we went for a little ski trip on the lake in order to loosen our muscles and to get rid of our headaches.

Our routine was the same during the next twenty-four hours. Nicolas had been gone for almost three days, but we would be able to hold out for another week with our freezer fish. It was cold and misty and sometimes razor-sharp ice crystals formed in the air.

As we were taking another short trip in the gloomy daylight we suddenly saw something that made us freeze in our tracks: there, over the ice, a huge Santa Claus was approaching. We stood still and watched him in fear and amazement. Like the monster we saw the

previous day, he seemed to be right in front of us. Again, we couldn't hear him and he didn't seem to be getting any closer. We hurried back to the igloo and when we looked around, Santa Claus was gone. A gust of wind had dispersed the mist and the large icefield stretched out clearly before us. Far away in the distance a tiny dot was approaching, and fifteen minutes later it proved to be Nicolas. He was carrying a big parcel. When he had put his baggage down we embraced him and told him about the monster and Santa Claus. He burst out laughing and said: "You've seen nothing more than a fox and me. Haven't you ever heard of light refraction? When there is a certain degree of humidity in the air, it causes small objects at the horizon to grow into gigantic shapes; it is a kind of mirage. But I have good news. A day and a half's journey from here is a settlement of Arctic gnomes. We have to get there as quickly as possible, because there is another snowstorm on its way. We will only take what we can carry. First, you have to put on these clothes that our Arctic brothers have provided us with."

He had all kinds of things with him: sealskin boots (the inner and outer soles were separated by a thin layer of dried grass); hare-wool socks; a shirt made of bird skin with down on the inside; a shiny pair of white pants made of sheared hare fur, which tucked into the boots. It all was topped by a beautiful, loosely fitting coat of sheared hare fur, with a deep fur hood attached that served as the pointed hat, and a pair of kid gloves. We felt like princes.

"But now I have to rest for a few hours because I am exhausted."

We entered the igloo, prepared a meal of flounder

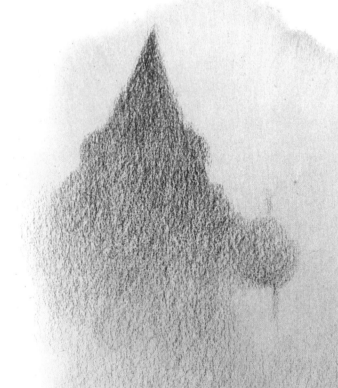

and nuts, and poured out a drink to celebrate our re-union in this barren country. Nicolas ate it all with gusto, including the fish! Then he lay down and slept soundly for five hours. Later he opened his eyes, got up, and said: "Let's go!"

We made our way along the high ice wall, climbing over it at a low point, and arrived on a vast icefield. The first part of the journey was terrible. Thousands of ice points and crevasses made skiing almost impossible. Sometimes Nicolas saw, in the same way as Arctic dogs can, hidden crevasses under the snow where we wouldn't have suspected anything; in order to get around them we had to backtrack for long distances. The frozen mud had broken off our skis completely. After many hours we began to descend and finally reached smoother ice with patches of snow.

The origin of the belief in Santa Claus can be explained as follows: in the wintry cold and snowy skies, the light refraction caused people from time to time to see ordinary gnomes who had taken on giant proportions.

While we were resting we asked Nicolas, "Where do Arctic gnomes get their fur from? They don't kill animals or eat meat or fish, do they?"

"Here they do eat them and use their fur," he said, "but they don't kill them. The gnomes have to rely on them because there is nothing else. They take what they need from the Arctic fox's winter store; the fox doesn't object, especially as gnomes don't need much."

Twelve hours later we approached another ice cliff. We could see igloos in the distance. The next minute a bunch of fur-clad gnomes were clicking toward us on snowshoes. They emitted wild cries and practically knocked us over embracing us, rubbing noses, and pinching us amicably. At the igloos we were about to creep in through the tunnel when a sort of letter opener was thrust at us for brushing off snow and ice particles from our fur clothing that might melt and then freeze again later with serious consequences.

This illustrates how small such a gnome igloo is.

The brushing of clothes can take up considerable time after journeys in snowstorms, and meanwhile it gives the one who enters time to call "Someone has arrived!"—thus assuring the observance of good manners.

The cone shape of a gnome cap serves to prevent his being flattened by loads of snow or other disasters from above, because objects simply glance off the sides.

We crept farther into the tunnel. Dexterous hands pulled our anoraks over our heads. We were in the main igloo around which the other smaller ones were built. The smaller ones were connected to the main one by tunnels so that the inhabitants could contact each other without going outside.

We were barely inside when the snowstorm prophesied by Nicolas broke in full force. A smoky fire was burning in the igloo. The few women inside had on nothing more than short pants, which startled us at first, but it was obviously the norm here. Quite soon the men undressed entirely. Two of them dragged legs of snow hare onto the platform of the igloo. It was apparent that they were preparing a party for us. The meat was boiled in pots and seal bacon bubbled in other vessels.

The men were smaller than us. They had black eyes and very black greasy hair. All had broad, oval faces. The women laughed constantly while they rapidly prepared the food with their small, well-shaped hands.

The large igloo was the meeting place for eating and dancing, and the gnome families apparently lived in the smaller igloos.

While we were waiting for the meal Nicolas said, "I will give you the basic rules for survival in the wilderness:

1. Water is always more important than food.
2. In intense cold always breathe through your nose, never through your mouth.
3. In extreme circumstances you can go without sleep for five days.
4. Travel in the late night hours and in early morning.
5. Panic is your worst enemy. With normal reserves you can withstand hunger, thirst, cold, heat, loneliness, fatigue, long distances, physical injury, and loss of blood for a long period. Panic always upsets the balance. Remain calm. Make the most of every situation.
6. If you have to undertake something, consider whether you: react quickly . . . or recklessly; are cautious . . . or only frightened; demand enough . . . or too much of yourself and others.
7. See to it that you are armed against scurvy in perpetual snow areas by daily drinking water in which pine twigs have been boiled. Take them along with you into icy areas.
8. Remember that snow is an excellent insulator. Look how sled dogs let themselves get snowed under right up to the tips of their noses (which they then cover with their bushy tails).
9. Frostbite begins with numbness. Pay attention to that. A frozen patch turns gray or whitish-yellow. Don't rub it! You'll break the skin. Warm your limb under your arm or thaw it in lukewarm water.
10. To orient yourself:
    Clouds above open water are dark gray,
    clouds above snow or ice are white,
    birds fly early in the morning from the land to the sea
    and in the evening from the sea to land
    (seagulls, puffins, and hunters).

This is all in the Secret Book!" he said. He showed it to us, as well as illustrations of a Yeti family and gnomes from far-off places.

Yeti, front view   Yeti, from behind

These are in fact
actual pictures of the
YETI or ABOMINABLE SNOWMAN

(which he doesn't want to exist at all!)
and he is a grand master at <u>not being seen</u>.

He is reproduced on the opposite page with
unnatural clarity.

This will give you
an idea of
the difference
in
body size:

Yeti   <u>Homo</u> <u>sapiens</u>   gnome

The ABOMINABLE SNOWWOMAN,
in spite of her superfluous milk
supply, switches rapidly to an
additional feeding for her small
Yeti (abominable snowchild)
of ice wafers, water ices,
ice creams, and frost
flowers, etc.

The Yeti normally walks upright.
If he thinks he is being observed he walks on all fours.

This is why Arctic and
Himalayan travelers have for
centuries thought that what
they saw was a polar bear.

He glides over frozen lakes
at enormous speeds.

GNOMES FROM OTHER LANDS

Karl May must have known the American Indian gnomes, but he didn't mention them.

The Arctic gnome, chief of the settlement, ↓ at -76°F.

Unfortunately the clothes louse (Pediculus vestimenti) can stand this temperature, and the head louse (Pediculus capitis) is cosily ensconced.

The Scots or loch gnome relies heavily upon whiskey to combat rheumatism.
He is friendly with the Loch Ness monster.

The Balinese or rice gnomes enliven the Emerald Belt with their dancing to a gamelan.

The venerable coolie gnome lives on two grains of rice daily!

It has been months since he had his last egg roll.

A Peruvian gnome in the icy, rarified air high in the mountains.

The blankets are made from llama or vicuña wool.

Sunbaked Australian or pouch gnomes used the boomerang long before the aborigines for friendly acrobatics and to get at rare berries in this barren land. The women have only one child at a time but can produce twice.

The bushman gnome obtains fruit from the trees with a three-pronged arrow.

His arms are too short to stretch the bow

so he must lie on his back to shoot.

The bushman gnome can be found all over Africa.

The Syrian gnomes
have kept the golden hamster
as a pet for thousands
of years.

This animal had
only been known in
western Europe
since 1931.

Hidden under the veil
is the exotic beauty
of the female.

The Papuan (New Guinea)
gnome is not the
friendliest sort. It could
be that not only his
nose bone
but also his costume
(that gets in his way
practically all the time)
contribute to his
ill humor.

An Orthodox Jewish gnome takes a turn with his Arabian brother after an endless wrangle over an orange consignment, although the wares have been tapped and felt and even cut open.

Greek → gnome, who after a good glass of ouzo and an ample portion of spanaki avgolimono (spinach with egg sauce), begins the Firtaki or Letkis (dances).

The Austrian gnome has to take off his plume when it snows or his cap would get top-heavy. A pair of knobby knees protrude from under his lederhosen.

It had not occurred to us on the flax fields at home —
there is lots of charm to be found in Holland, our own
sweet little country:

the roguish
Volendammer

the reserved, shy
but pleasant
Staphorst woman
who can only
sing semibreves.

← two →
merry Zeeland
variations

a Bunschoten - Spakenburg beauty
who can't help
smelling slightly
of fish from
the nearby
sea.

When we were finally seated in a circle and about to begin the meal, the oldest gnome said that he hoped we were not too hungry because the meat was of an inferior quality, actually not fit to set before guests, more like dog meat. Nicolas appeared to be au fait with the rules of the game as he immediately said that we were certainly not hungry and had just dropped by for the company. The old gnome cut a slice of meat, tasted it, chewed it, and said: "Just as I said—worthless meat, half-rotten and badly prepared. I don't dare to give it to you!" He had barely uttered the words when everyone dove into the food. Deep into the night we devoured the finest legs of hare and legs of duck, and then alternated with seal bacon. The criticism of the food was a sort of courtesy ritual. We glistened with grease from head to toe and could hardly utter a word. During the meal we had heard numerous stories about living in snow and ice that only increased our respect for these friendly, cheerful gnomes who considered hospitality their ultimate duty.

It turned out that although everyone was happily naked, the clothes Nicolas had brought for us were the same as theirs. Finally we went off to bed. We were each allotted a separate small igloo, and not without reason: two husbands put their wives at our disposal as a generous gesture, a custom that one could not refuse at this latitude without offending someone, so we left it at that.

The storm was still raging when we awoke. We were assured that it would last three or four days, and there was no chance of journeying farther. We spent the days chatting, listening to old tales, and watching how the Arctic gnomes ran their households. As a toy they use a *snorrebot:* a piece of bone or button with two holes is threaded with two strings. Once it gets going it keeps whirring around as long as the threads are rhythmically extended and retracted.

Seeing the women sewing fur was fascinating. They cut pieces from a skin with a small knife that had a handle in the center. Tanning was done by chewing the hide. The pieces were assembled without any measuring and were sewn together with a bone needle and a thread of walrus hide. When it was ready no seam was evident in the shorn fur, and the garment was always a perfect fit. Precision in sewing together the fur pieces is of vital importance as a split seam can let so much cold through in a storm that frostbite might result.

We spent the days reading their Secret Book and getting ours up to date. The storm did indeed begin to abate after the third day. On the fourth day it was suddenly absolutely still. We all went outside and had a

good stretch. This time we were lucky: blue and violet streaks adorned the evening sky and yellow-green and soft reddish tints marked the horizon. The famous northern lights (aurora borealis), which occur because sun-born electrons and protons bombard the oxygen and nitrogen molecules in our atmosphere, revealed themselves in all their beauty.

Suddenly we noticed that the gnomes seemed to be looking at something we could not see. Nicolas stood beside us and laughed: "There goes our lift to Cork III!"

When we looked at him inquiringly, he said, "Look carefully! Don't you see anything?"

We peered intently. After a long time we saw a vague shape. "Quite!" said Nicolas. "That is a Yeti."

"But aren't they only found in the Himalayas?"

"There are more of them in the world than you think. They can make themselves invisible; no human has ever seen one."

The oldest gnome had come to stand next to us. "Would you ask the Yeti if he could take us to Cork III?" asked Nicolas. We skied behind the old gnome toward the body disappearing in the distance and in half an hour we had caught up with him.

The Yeti stood still. The old gnome bowed and said, "Good evening, Zero. Haven't seen you for a long time. How is Frigida and little Ice Cream?"

The gigantic figure made no reply and regarded us suspiciously. Eventually he said in a deep voice, "Those look like two people. Are you sure I won't risk being discovered?"

"I guarantee that personally," said the Arctic gnome, while Nicolas growled in our ear: "They have one-track minds—fear of being seen."

"All right then," said Zero, "although I don't relish taking risks."

A quarter of an hour later we had reached an agreement: he would take us to Altay, five hundred miles to the southeast, the following evening.

"And I don't want you to see how I walk,'" he said, "even though you are gnomes. I have an old blanket at home and you'll go into that."

He stuck to his words. He came rumbling along the following evening carrying a grayish-red blanket. A long farewell to the gnomes then took place while Zero spread the blanket on the ice. When we eventually stood on the blanket, Nicolas said, "Where did you get this blanket? It seems familiar!"

"I found it a hundred years ago as I was on the way home from north Tibet, after visiting my nephews and nieces in the Himalayas."

"Good Lord," said Nicolas, "that is one of Nikolai Przhevalsky's blankets. He has indeed been to north Tibet . . . I'll tell you about it on the way."

Zero pulled the blanket around us and held it by the four corners so we sat in a cozy hole. We were at his mercy. "Nothing to fear," said Nicolas. "Yetis are absolutely reliable." It was pitch black in the blanket and it didn't smell terribly fresh. We seemed to be traveling at a high speed. "Yes, old Przhevalsky," said Nicolas. "I saw him enter Mongolia from Kyakhta in November 1871. He was a tough, testy rascal, and he traveled with camels. He stayed in Mongolia for three years and came as far as north Tibet. That was where his camels gave out from exhaustion. It so happened that I was there and slept in his tent. We could not get fresh camels so on my advice he switched to yaks. A yak is a mountain creature without parallel. It can go to an altitude of twenty thousand feet and can follow mountain paths with a burden of 250 pounds beside precipices even difficult for mountain goats and sheep—all without one slip of a hoof.

"Przhevalsky* had to return because of a lack of funds. He was the one who discovered the horse that is named after him, and the wild camel. He must have lost this blanket somewhere on the way.

"This is in any case a strange way of traveling! We gnomes have other means of transport."

The wild yak lives at altitudes up to twenty thousand feet. The bull weighs up to 2,000 pounds, the cow 880. Hair: long blackish-brown. Tame yak: bull up to 1,500 pounds, cow 770. Color: light to spotted. Milk: thick and creamy. Yaks can be ridden. In snowstorms they remain so still that they appear dead.

yak

Przewalski paard

Nicolai
Michailowitoch
Przewalski

* Nikolai M. Przhevalsky, 1839–1888, Russian general. Made four voyages of discovery through Asia and Tibet, and charted part of it.

Troika, elk, and Arctic fox
are not the only
means of transportation!

When weather conditions
are propitious, the gnomes
make fifteen-mile night marches
on foot,

easily taking in stride the load
of a sled filled with nuts

↓

or of a wood chick.
The old knapsack and the
basket filled with
fruit, which they
carry on their backs,
don't slow them down
at all.

For quick shopping trips,

they use the walking bicycle (eleven thousand years old),

and for slow trips the rather trite wheelbarrow; ↑

for larger loads they use the freight tricycle; ↑

and for an owl chick that has fallen ← out of its nest, they use the carrying sled.

A gnome likes to keep his feet dry.

From a standing position he can easily jump thirty inches, just like a frog, and with a run, he can jump almost eight feet!

Should the brush or the sogginess on a river bank prevent a run, he will vault with a pole over incredible distances and land on the other side

dry as a cork.

The otter (see GNOMES) is a faithful ferryman.

Floats are assembled without a nail.

Although the gnome hates to swim, it is sometimes necessary.

The belt is useful for keeping clothes and baggage dry.

Even in snow and ic[e]
the gnome does not
sink (except in so[ft]
melting snow)
and is not
held up.

Downhill skiing
and
ski-jumping
are his favorite ways
of getting about.

If it is getting late, he whistles for a pheasant.

Then there is the cargo sleigh in all forms and the prick sleigh (sometimes you can see the pinpricks in the snow by looking carefully).

Ice dancing is very much in vogue.

Unencumbered by knots, ropes,
picks, etc., the gnome goes up
and down the steepest slopes.
He goes down quicker than up:
  without tacking,
  he makes use
  of every unevenness
  with his stick
  and descends
  in a straight
  line.

Air travel

is for long journeys or for
flying over young plantations
to examine choked rivers, floods,
and to take note of decreases
or increases in green.
Usually the whole family
makes a day of it.

The stork provides trustworthy transport

though only in spring and summer.

—

The misconception that newborn babies are delivered by the stork is a result of faulty observation.

Not all the well-meant offers
of a lift can be accepted.

The reasons are obvious:
the tortoise is too slow to
be of much use,
a lift on a hedgehog
doesn't work,

and a
squirrel is
full of fleas.

It makes no difference to
the gnome whether
← it's light
or dark. →
He sees everything.

Even in dark passages under the ground (earthman)
he knows his way.

If he wants to cross a field unseen he just
tunnels through the snow with his sharply
pointed cap
(to practiced observers his trail is
quite clear).

If necessary the gnome can do this
in loose earth
↓

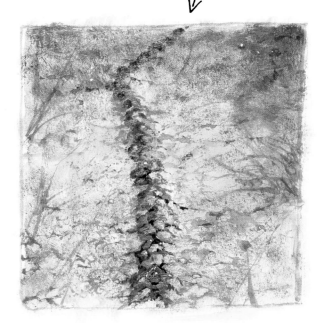

but too often these shallow
runs are considered mole
furrows, so you can't be
careful enough before setting
out a mole trap!

(travelogue continued)

We became drowsy and have no recollection of the following hours or days. The Yeti probably tried to confuse us and the next thing we heard was, "Here it is," as he put the blanket down on the ground. When we stepped out we saw a mound with a rough gate in front of us. The words "III Balon" were chalked on the wall. Zero had delivered us at the Altay station.

The Yeti did not feel at ease at all. He kept looking around shyly and muttering, "Not to be seen! Be gone. Too many people."

"Shall I make you a large igloo so you can rest?" asked Nicolas. "Then you can creep away." But the Yeti disappeared without a word. Nicolas shrugged and knocked at the door. A troll's wife appeared.

"Good day, Boney," Nicolas said. "Isn't Cork III at home?"

"Cork sick!" she said.

"This is Cork III's original family hole. He and his wife kicked out their family after their conversion," Nicolas said to us. It was a genuine troll's den inside. A river ran through it and there were barred cells for stolen children. Two balloons hung on the ceiling. A corpulent troll lay in the corner on fir branches. When we stood near him he held his stomach, groaning. We uncovered his stomach and examined him.

"General constipation from overeating," Nicolas said. "Nothing serious. He must be properly purged."

He showed us how to make an enema-syringe and told us about a folk remedy used for such purposes. When everything was prepared, the troll's wife adminis-

tered the apparatus. At first nothing happened. After a quarter of an hour Cork III rose from his couch and ran outside, leaving the door open. Within seconds there were noises from the forest that approached explosions. "Give him time," Nicolas said, closing the door fastidiously.

It was eight o'clock and we were hungry. Nicolas rustled up all sorts of edibles from a cupboard and made us feel we were back in the civilized world instead of in the middle of the Siberian taiga. At least we were far from the icy Arctic region and we could use a balloon again, although Nicolas had not given any indication of what was awaiting us at the Yenisey.

Cork III came back from the forest half an hour later, white around the gills and with beads of sweat on his low forehead but obviously relieved. Nicolas got him to

take a balloon outside and an hour later we were air-
borne in a moderate wind on the way to Crown Cork on
the Yenisey River near Pit-Gorodok, in the Yeniseyskiy
range.

The journey to Crown Cork went well. It took three
days and was uneventful. We once drifted over a bare
hill where an extraordinarily small moose had scraped
the snow aside and stood eating moss. He and Nicolas
exchanged greetings.

"That is One Eye, the dwarf," Nicolas said. "He has
been called that since he was a calf. I found him half-
dead in a river when he was four months old. The mosquitos had overwhelmed him, which happens here

sometimes. His eyes, nose, mouth, and ears were filled
with mosquitos, and they had bitten everything into a
bleeding mass. He had waded into the water to get rid of
them, though it didn't help much. I cleaned him up as
much as possible but his left eye couldn't be saved, so I
had to remove it. He didn't seem to be growing at all. I
managed to ferret out his mother, who had abandoned
him, and she had just enough milk in her udder to suckle
him."

Balloon Station IV was larger than the previous
three; we met some tall, broad-shouldered gnomes waiting for a favorable wind.

We put on our skis again, ready to cross the snow-
covered landscape. Crown Cork was a very old troll

The wolverene (Gulo gulo), *also called glutton or rock cat, is a mountain marten in the extreme north measuring up to three feet long. Its pelt is highly prized by the Siberians because breath does not condense inside it.*

without a tail. He wore a pair of owllike spectacles that probably had plain glass in them. Still, Nicolas said, he could read a few words and he had concocted a timetable that was pretty useless since everything depended on the wind. He behaved as if he were indispensable even for the minutest trifles and even fussed around with our skis till Nicolas commanded him to stop.

After this we left for Nicolas's house twenty-five miles away. The snowy taiga was most impressive and we crossed all kinds of animal tracks; we even saw a sable marten and a wolverene.

Circling a village in rather a wide sweep, we came across a roebuck in a trap. He was still alive but was crazed from fear and pain. Nicolas tried to calm him

down so that we could climb onto his neck and saw through the steel snare, but he kept struggling and pulling away, thereby tightening the cord.

It was a terrible sight. Blood and froth came out of the roebuck's mouth and he was thrashing about so wildly he seemed on the verge of madness. When he had calmed down a bit from sheer exhaustion we quickly climbed near the snare and took turns sawing. Two of us held the snare away from the skin while the third sawed. It was not easy to get through the plaited steel wires and the still-struggling buck was a frightful hindrance. When we reached the next-to-the-last wire, Nicolas sent us down because the buck was sure to bolt away.

The snare had barely snapped off when he made a desperate dash for freedom. With a thud Nicolas was thrown against a tree and lay there motionless. As we knelt next to him, he said without batting an eyelid, "That's a broken leg! Help take the boot off."

His shin was indeed broken. It was one of the rare cases of an animal injuring a gnome, though done inadvertently. We were surrounded by cedars, firs, spruce, birch, and mountain ash, but no elder for a splint, so we had to make do with a pair of smooth mountain-ash branches. We couldn't find arnica in the snow either, to speed up the healing. One of us pulled at the broken leg until the soles were level, while the other put the mountain-ash branches around the limb and tied them securely. It must have been agony; Nicolas did not utter a word but indulged in a few stiff swigs of brandy. We then cut off his sock and boot and bound them around his foot to keep it warm.

The Siberian roe is much bigger than the European, although it has a six-tined antler.

We were still ten miles from his home. We cut branches from a willow farther on from which we could make a stretcher and braces for ourselves. Our knapsack belts were strong enough to support the whole thing.

Nicolas growled approvingly when all was ready. We put our skis on and tried to start off gingerly. It was difficult at first and we fell a couple of times, causing scathing words from the stretcher, but gradually we managed to cover some distance. Nicolas pointed the way. Two hours later we stood under an enormous cedar that hid the entrance to his house. Just as we were about to carry him in he said, "Wait. We will never get through the revolving door like this. Get my wife."

We entered the cave, walked through a long passage, and knocked. The buxom Siberian woman who answered raced with us outside. Nicolas was standing up. She hugged him and said, "My little bear, what has happened to you?" Her name was Sofia Wladimirowna. Nicolas insisted on hobbling in. He was put to bed and we took the splints off his leg, rubbed the skin with arnica ointment, and made better splints from elder branches.

During the meal that followed he said: "I shall now put an end to your uncertainty. My compatriots were angry enough with you because of the Siberian passages in your first book to summon you to court. The journey to Lapland was enough to satisfy the western gnomes, but thereafter we wanted you in Siberia. At first Mirko

was against it but he gave in when the king insisted. I had to meet you in Lapland and bring you here to study your behavior in my capacity as justice of the peace. At first uncertainty made me rude, for which I offer my apologies. The king also forbade us to let you see the whole Secret Book. You have not grumbled although you must have been consumed with curiosity to know what was going to happen; that has not passed unnoticed. In a secret message received at Crown Cork, I was given the freedom to decide whether you should be prosecuted or not; the help you gave me with my leg was the decisive factor. I have recommended that the court case be canceled. You may return home, but on three conditions. Those I shall tell you when your exhausted bodies have had eight hours sleep."

Somewhat confused, we stumbled into bed. Sofia, who seemed to think we had more or less saved her husband's life, tucked us in herself, although we were so tired we hardly noticed it.

We woke, still not completely rested, and were very soon sitting down for breakfast when Nicolas said, "And now the three conditions! One: you must take back all the dreadful things you said about Siberians in your next book. Two: you will have to complete a couple of competence tests. Three: you will take home a commission. You will be taken to a special address. I shall say nothing more than that."

We felt both melancholy and excited. What was going to happen now? Nicolas silently shook hands. When we asked if this was goodbye, he said nothing.

Sofia led us to a cave high in the mountain and left us there. We walked through a passage and reached a door decorated with a closed eye. When we knocked, the eye opened.

The door opened by itself and a big gnome with a broad smile stood in front of us. Peace radiated from his face. He said in a friendly voice: "Quite. The Dutch guests. Nicolas sent a message to expect you. Welcome to Morpheus's arms. I am the Sandman."

The Sandman in the middle of Siberia? To say we were surprised would be an understatement!

The Sandman's face was like an autumny golden apple with thousands of little wrinkles. When we were seated in easy chairs in the living room we asked him how he managed his sleep deliveries. He would not tell us but apparently it had something to do with magic stratospheric motions that included the fourth dimension. "Just as time stands still on the edge of a black hole in the universe, so I let people drop off into timelessness," he said simply.

Later on we were allowed to take a look in his cellars, where innumerable sacks of sleep sand were piled. On some were written: "Requisites for HIBERNATION."

"Don't you have to leave to put people to sleep?" we asked.

"No," he said. "Some nights everyone has to fend for himself. I can't always be out. I'm too old. I'm as old as the world."

He told us a couple of wonderful but terribly tiring stories about famous people who had trouble falling asleep, until we became so sleepy we nearly fell off our chairs. Then with sand in our eyes we went to a wonderful bed some hours too early, embraced by the arms of Morpheus.

THE FIRST MISSION

We awoke in a tropical valley between green mountains. It was sunset and stifling hot. Where and in which time were we?

There was not a soul around to ask. We deliberated with heavy hearts. We were probably expected to do something, but what? Perhaps we had been dropped in a deserted spot to see if we remembered the rules of survival. A river ran below us. Since we had to go somewhere, it seemed wise to follow it downstream (Nicolas had taught us to do that when lost), and even more so because the water was low and it was easy walking on river sand. We were accompanied by swarms of biting mosquitos and other flying small fry. Two crows circled high above the mountains. We made ourselves a shield against the mosquitos by tucking grass blades under the rims of our pointed caps, and we kept our hands under our beards. We suddenly noticed the gnome sign for danger in the stones on the bank: DANGER! GO TO THE LEFT! So gnomes had definitely been here! The only problem was that if we went left, our path would lead straight to the mountains and we would be completely lost. In addition, the sign looked years old and since there seemed little chance of meeting a gnome in the mountains, we decided to go gingerly on.

Since time immemorial the gnomes have worked with secret branch signals in forest and field – for example,

"general danger signal"

←

" go 300 yards to the right"

"search from right to left and back" →

or

"look out for the troll's snare"
↓

a pinecone sewn into
    an oak branch is almost
        as stupid as
          the troll himself,

and just as ridiculous as a
    pheasant cock with the tail of a blackcock
         ↓

(not that it has
  anything to do with
a gnome,
but it just came to mind).

gnome signs

... or a woodcock with a drake's tail,

or a roe deer with mountain goat's horns,

or a fox with boar's teeth,

a rabbit with a long tail,

a magpie with the comb and wattle of a common or garden rooster,

a wild boar with roebuck antlers

or an innocent mother duck with the tail of a pheasant!

that sort of thing

We had not gone three hundred feet before we stupidly tumbled into a pit with vertical rock walls that had been hidden under the white river sand.

At dawn we found ourselves, black-and-blue, looking out of a cage at a sort of beardless Neolithic man who wore a loincloth and a necklace of yellow eye teeth. He picked up the cage, shook us savagely, and gave a coarse laugh. Then we were put against the wall of the living-room cell. A couple of silent women were at work and a slavish little man brought us a thick meat porridge, which we had to share with a mouse. In a niche in the rock opposite we saw a gnome couple standing on a shelf. They look disheveled and miserable.

"Hey, pssst!" the man called in gnome language. "Where have you come from?"

"From the Sandman in Siberia."

He looked at us skeptically.

"Can't you get us out of the cage?" we asked.

"We are stuck to this shelf," said the woman dismally, "and must stand in this weather house. We are the last gnomes in this country. Jaw has eaten them all or chased them away." (A witch predicted at Jaw's birth that he, the chief, would remain without children until the gnomes came to his salvation.)

The man said, "All his wives are childless. He had all the gnomes in the country rounded up and at first beseeched them to help, questioned them, then tortured them, and finally conceived the primitive plan of fattening them up and eating them in the hope of getting their potency tranferred to him. You also will be stuffed and eaten."

One of the women threw a cloth over our cage to prevent us from talking to the gnomes. By morning we had figured out a solution. When the cloth was removed at porridge-time we told Jaw we could help him with his problem. It took hours to gain his confidence until at last he agreed to our suggestions, which was that he arrange for women above child-bearing age to urinate in a stone pot. If we were freed and promised that we would not try to escape, we would arrange the rest.

We carved a primitive injection syringe from a tropical hardwood, steamed the urine gently over a low fire,
and injected Jaw's hard bottom with it three times a
week. The needle was much too thick, but these tough
rascals were used to pain. It must be said for Jaw that he
willingly underwent the treatment and became con-
vinced that our cure would work! When Jaw's youngest
wife became pregnant he was ecstatic. We could do
nothing wrong. Our first request was that he set free the
gnome couple from the weather house—they had to
learn to walk again, poor things, but they recovered
satisfactorily. Then we demanded that all other gnomes
be allowed to return safely, without retribution, and they
soon came back from the surrounding countryside. But
we had not seen the last of Jaw. Although we had taught
the wizard of the tribe how to administer the injections,
Jaw insisted that we assist at the birth of his first child.
We accompanied him on all his forays in the meantime
and we saw elephants, lions, tigers, antelopes, and
camels.

The heat, the mosquitos, the endless bloody battles
with neighboring tribes, and the beating to death of bi-
sons, and even worse, the trapping of mammoths—it all
became unbearable. We spent many a wakeful hour
working out how to leave without breaking our word.

Suddenly we awoke quite peacefully in bed at the
Sandman's home. His laughing eyes were peering at us

under the canopy and he said: "That was an easy commission for modern Westerners in a primitive land, wasn't it? Stupid of you to ignore the sign. Good that you kept your word. I called you back because it lasted more than three months—although that counted only as three days here."

That night he explained the essence of sleep, which is based on the interaction between the formatio reticularis and the gray matter, and it was scientifically indisputable. Then he told us the story of Sleeping Beauty—of the slumbering castle within impenetrable thorn hedges—in such a way that even Gustave Doré could not have illustrated more vividly. Then he told Snow White and the Seven Dwarfs, Rumpelstiltskin, and many others—always in the same fascinating fashion.

"You see," he explained, "a gnome was a perfectly normal being in the misty past when most fairy tales were created. Do you know that gnomes played an important part in recording fairy tales? Fairy tales are poeticized ancient wishes and experiences. Wrong must be punished; prisoners or bewitched must be freed; ugliness turned to beauty; dragons made harmless; stupidity and cruelty overcome. The small and clever become leaders and the gigantic become helpless. Just what we gnomes have always done.

"Naturally gnomes appear in countless stories, but since they are passed on by word of mouth—hardly anyone could read or write then—the gnome has become rather mutilated or disposed of altogether. Don't forget that many tales began in the last Stone Age and in the pre–Indo-Germanic cultures. You need not think they were created for children either! They sprang up among adults whose mental development was that of the children today. The adults listened with cocked ear and dreamy eye just as our children do."

Later he said, "Naturally our subconscious or, if you like, unconscious plays an enormous part in fairy tales, usually using the imagery of a lake or impenetrable forest. These two are symbols of the unknown dangerous world where past, present, and future are entangled and anything is possible. It is the fact that it is perfectly ordinary lake or forest that makes it so plausible. Anything you believe in exists. In your heart things are living realities so that you have no difficulty in placing them outside yourself in any landscape or surrounding. In short, you see what you want to see. If you were staying longer I'd show you around our fairy-tale world because it is so riveting, but I'll have to send that part of the Secret Book to you in Holland."

Toward morning, when our eyes had become heavy with sleep, he told a story of a very poor woodchopper and his wife and seven sons. "But that is the story of Tom Thumb!" we exclaimed.

"Of course! But Tom Thumb was not a human being. Here again we come across a corruption of words. Tom Thumb was a gnome, and none other that the famous gnome Thyme. So it was really Little Tom Thyme. I did mention once to Charles Perrault—I believe it was in 1697—that a human infant could never be only six inches tall, but he insisted on making him in his story into a little human boy. He also said that he felt embarrassed about these fairy tales, and that he only wrote them for fun, and even then under the name of his son. He thought that nobody would ever read them anyway, because of the fact that he was really a scholar."

THE SECOND MISSION

We woke up in a country laid waste by a werewolf. Villages were burned to the ground, cattle killed or stolen, game poached, people terrorized. It was the fifteenth century. The desperate population was paralyzed with fear and superstition, aggravated by the fact that the werewolf attacked at night in various places simultaneously. We were dropped in the wilderness at the edge of the country from which the beast undertook his forays and where for years no one had dared set foot. We searched for footprints but found only those of humans.

We were lucky the second night: from our tree hideout we saw the creature walking over a clearing. There was not one but three of them, and they were men with bewitched wolfskins! Since they thought no one was watching, the rogues walked upright and talked softly to one another. After this it was child's play for us: we made

a trap with homemade barbed wire stretched over it. When they came from the wilderness the next day, we attracted their attention while they were walking upright and got them to run after us once they realized that we had discovered their secret. We lured them on, walked over the trap without setting it off (we weighed so little), and waited on the other side. With ghastly curses they fell into the depths, their wolfskins remaining caught on the barbed wire.

The next day the trio was rendered harmless by two strong men and the skins were burned.

When we again awoke at the Sandman's, he came and sat on the edge of our bed and said: "Better, each time better! Almost real gnomes."

He was holding a section of the Secret Book that we had not seen. "Look," he said as he pointed to two papers sticking out of the book. "Read it!" He opened up the passages and we followed his wrinkled finger with burning curiosity: "In the warm age before the last ice age about a hundred and thirty thousand years before the last era, the gnomes tamed the savage Jaw, to the salvation of the gnomes in Asia."

Everything was minutely recorded even including our names. Farther on was the story of the werewolf in the Middle Ages. We were speechless, and the Sandman laughed at our reaction. "So you see," he said, "this should make the difficult journey to Siberia worthwhile. You had to come all the way here because I'm the only one who could put you into such a deep sleep that you could wander freely around in the past and have the opportunity to earn your honorable mention in the Secret Book!"

THE THIRD MISSION

After breakfast the Sandman pensively filled a pipe. He poured three glasses of wine. "You are about to leave," he said, giving us a wide smile. "You stood up well to the two tests to which we subjected you, but they were merely exercises. The third and most difficult test lies ahead." His face suddenly lost all its laughter lines and he said softly, "There once was a spirit in a bottle—a puny, naked, powerless spirit. He was well stored in his bottle for ages, but people let him out and now he has become a Dragon with Seven Heads. If you don't succeed in making this world-threatening monster harmless, annihilation will result."

We still did not understand what he was driving at.

"The time for the General Alarm has arrived," said the Sandman. "We tread ever narrower paths beside ever deeper precipices. The monster I mean is the DRAGON OF POLLUTION.

"Its first head is called LET THE FUTURE TAKE CARE OF ITSELF; the second, IT WILL LAST MY LIFETIME; the third, IGNORANCE IS BLISS; the fourth, AFTER US, THE DELUGE; the fifth, LET'S WAIT TILL IT HAPPENS; the sixth, IT WON'T BE ALL THAT BAD; and the seventh, COULDN'T CARE LESS."

He began to pace the room, overcome by emotion. We kept quiet. He was right. The end of the world seemed to be advancing with giant strides.

"Every gift has a plug attached," he resumed, "every utensil devours energy; nearly every river in the world has been poisoned; the oceans are filled with radioactive refuse packed in containers that will rust within a few years; the freon in aerosol sprays contaminates the stratosphere; drivers are fined for throwing garbage out of the window but not for the dangerous gases that escape from their exhaust pipes! A factory is allowed to turn a romantic brook into a black, muddy stream! I begin to wonder who is mad?"

He became more and more distressed. We could hardly recognize him. "What I observe around me is pollution of the water, depletion of the ground, suffocation of the air. Hundreds of square miles of forests disappear daily in three of the five continents; it is not only disastrous for the oxygen supply of the whole world but also for the preservation of numerous animal species that will one day only exist in zoos as poor shadows of their former selves."

He calmed down somewhat, sat down, and looking squarely at us, said, "This is your greatest battle and at the same time the commission to which you will have to dedicate the rest of your lives: call a halt to this dragon, drive him back, destroy him, or your children's children will have no future.

"This is what your situation is at present: as Nicolas already told you, we intended to take you to court and to punish you by, for example, not making you big again. I have recommended dropping that plan and giving you this mission instead. We gained confidence in you after Nicolas's report on the journey, and that simplified matters for us.

"Just as it was Mirko's job to get you to Lapland and Nicolas's to take you to the Yenisey, so it is mine, as oldest gnome in the world, to share this burden with you: reduce the number and the needs of spoiled humanity. Practice the methods you have learned from the gnomes. THIS is the essential call of the gnomes!

"Go now," he said at the end of the night. "Sleep once more in my house the sleep of the just, but then go into the world and destroy the Dragon with Seven Heads. Let no obstacle stand in your way. The present direction humanity is taking will lead into an abyss. Return! Reform!"

He went through the door carrying a candlestick and said: "Slitzweitz. May you prosper!"

THE RETURN

It was morning when we awoke, damp and shivering, having slept restlessly for twenty-four hours in a sort of slumber full of nightmares about monsters and calamities. In a wooden room, we lay naked on the floor on top of our old clothes and covered over by the duffel coats in which we had come. A stove glowed in a corner, and we got a glimpse of an unknown taiga outside. As we put our clothes on we noticed that the floor seemed a long way below us and we felt the empty place on our heads. We were normal adults again. A note lay on the table: "Follow the rising sun until one o'clock. Then you will see a village on the other side of the Yenisey. The ice is safe. Use your gnome's wisdom to avoid cracks! Once on the other side look for the fifth house from the left. Farewell! Nicolas."

Our luggage stood in the corner. Nothing was missing. We found two piles of rubles and our book, also enlarged as well as our—same size—Arctic clothes and our old pointed caps, neatly folded flat.

Our hearts were heavy and we felt disoriented. This was the irrevocable end to the most intimate contact humans had ever had with gnomes. Yet there was nothing we could do about it. We had to start, so we went out and closed the door behind us.

We were not even three hundred feet from the hut before we heard some forest workers. Since we became gnome-still, they did not see us and went noisily into a wooden shed. We walked on. The forest was one plantation, but the trunks were not close together. Our only guide was the sun, which had started as a fiery ball and then gradually faded but remained visible through the treetops.

The first rays of light filtered weakly through the trees, and we set our course by the sun as instructed by Nicolas from his sickbed. Without meaning to we found ourselves proceeding cautiously at first because we were not accustomed to being so far above the ground and could not judge every bush or snow bubble as accurately. We were also inclined to bend far forward to prevent our pointed caps from being knocked off by branches and twigs.

Nicolas, who had arranged absolutely everything, including winding our watches, must have known it would be a cloudless day.

We saw signs of wild ponies. We followed their trail, which went in our general direction until it veered to the left, preventing us from asking them for a ride.

We then followed the spoor of a moose. We got near him by moving soundlessly, but when he realized we were there he crashed off.

We understood sadly: the intimate contact we had shared with nature for so many weeks, whereby we could naturally communicate with all animals, was gone forever.

A little farther on was a clearing in the forest. Four roe deer stood near trees on the far side. Had we still been gnomes, we could have approached near enough to admire their slender brown-gray figures, but now they fled with high leaps. We were once again members of the two-legged race that they were quite justified in fearing.

Our luggage seriously hampered us in the deep snow (by our increased gravity; as gnomes we had become too used to not sinking into the snow). Nicolas had even taken this delay into account: the forest only went on till one o'clock! We stood at the top of a long slope. The broad, frozen Yenisey lay below us, its banks lined with bare scrub. We could make out a village on the far side. When we climbed down to the river and onto the icefield, we even saw tire tracks. We began the long crossing. So this was the Yenisey, one of the mightiest Siberian rivers, which empties into the Arctic Ocean.

In olden times this was a paradise for capercaillies, causing the banks to be "black" with them, but now they are largely poached. In spite of the rows of the horrible, baitless, razor-sharp hooks of the fish poachers, the depths under the ice must still house masses of sturgeon, Thymallis, Coregonus (salmon), trout, and pike. We climbed the bank on the other side and saw a village of mostly small houses and a few larger ones. We passed a sleigh and a few people who gave us inquisitive looks but who said nothing, and stopped at the fifth house. A man wearing a uniform cap stood some way away glaring at us suspiciously. The wooden house was surrounded by a well-cared-for winter garden, and all was enclosed by a wooden fence. As we approached, the door half opened. An elderly woman motioned to us.

When we were close enough, she pulled us inside quickly and closed the door. While we waited in the hall she anxiously peered at the man in the street through a window in the front. Finally she came back and said in broken German that everything was fine. She led us to the first and only story, where there were two freshly

Nastassja
Filipowna

made beds, a bowl of water, and some soap. We put down our luggage, freshened ourselves up, and went downstairs. Our hostess was more relaxed now. Her name was Natasha Filipowna. She had a delicious borscht for us with black bread and a glass of beer. We were as hungry as hunters. It appeared from the conversation that the gnomes had arranged things here also: we were at a distant spur of the Trans-Siberian railway, the famous TransSib founded by the Czar Nicholas II, that connects Moscow with Vladivostok and is over six thousand miles long. We had to wait four days before there was a connection from the village in Achinsk with the TransSib, but that was the only inconvenience.

Our tickets home were all in order, as were our travel permits with stamps and all passports, and handwritten identity cards. The gnomes must have had friends even in this country. We had enough rubles for the days we were to spend on the train. Natasha told us that in order to avoid any possible trouble we would not be allowed to go into the street during these four days—the less attention we attracted, the better.

Thus we spent the next four days. Natasha looked after everything and we were content. Her late husband had been an interpreter for German prisoners during the war and she had picked up a few words. Her five children were married and lived far away. During these four days we finished our entire book and decided to offer it for publication to Jan Weggemans when we returned.

We had a long journey in front of us, and the Sandman's last words echoed in our ears. When we finally got home we would have to take his commission seriously. But even without the commission, our lives would never be the same after this unbelievable summons of the gnomes. Although we had gradually become used to our height and no longer bowed our heads to get through a door, we were still gnomes at heart. The fact that we had actually been gnomes could never be changed, even though we would soon be with our dear ones where we belonged.

While working on our book in the room upstairs in
Natasha's house we often caught each other staring out
at the vast taiga and the ice masses of the mighty Yenisey
in the distance, or pensively balancing our pointed caps
on the top of an index finger and letting them run along
the edge of the table; then, words were superfluous.

On a still, overcast day with a temperature just above freezing, we boarded the train, a symbol of bonds torn asunder. We had heard nothing more from the gnomes, though we could rest assured that they followed our doings closely. The endless trunks of the southern taiga began to slip past. There were long empty vistas deep into the forest, but we knew that trusted animals were housed there—and gnomes.

When we looked back through the window at the disappearing station shrouded in snow and mist, we thought we saw a red mark in the snow, from which, although we were ordinary people again, we received a forceful wireless message that amounted to Cicero's famous sigh:

QUO USQUE TANDEM?
How long still?